If God Loves Me, Why This?

If God
Loves Me,
Why This?

Finding Peace
in God's Plan for Us

Kim A. Nelson

Foreword by Stephen E. Robinson

DESERET
BOOK

Salt Lake City, Utah

DESERET BOOK is a registered trademark of Deseret Book Company.

Visit us at DeseretBook.com

Library of Congress Cataloging-in-Publication Data

Nelson, Kim A.
   If God loves me, why this? : finding peace in God's plan for us / Kim A. Nelson.
     p. cm.
   Includes index.
   ISBN-13: 978-1-59038-715-3 (hardback : alk. paper)
   ISBN-10: 1-59038-715-5 (hardback : alk. paper)
   1. Consolation. 2. Suffering—Religious aspects—Mormon Church.
3. Church of Jesus Christ of Latter-day Saints—Doctrines. 4. Mormon Church—Doctrines. I. Title.
   BX8643.C67N45 2007
   248.8'6—dc22
                                                              2006037086

Printed in the United States of America
Edwards Brothers Incorporated, Ann Arbor, MI

10   9   8   7   6   5   4   3   2   1

*I dedicate this book with respect and affection
to those who made it possible:
my wife, Lois; Jane Pugh; and Emily Watts.
The honest criticism and unwavering belief and support
of these sweet friends have made this old sow's ear
feel like a silk purse. Thank you.*

Contents

Foreword

Even the most skillfully drawn and perfectly detailed maps in the world are useless to us unless we can first locate ourselves upon them. Until the squiggly lines on the paper correspond to our experience of a larger reality, they may have value, but they have no meaning. They can be prized as artifacts, but they cannot be followed to find one's way. It has been said truly that the gospel is a map of mortality designed to show us the way home to our loving Heavenly Father. Unfortunately, until we know where we are in mortality—as opposed to where we think we are or even where we wish we were—we will find even the gospel to be a map that does not correspond to the realities of our lives, to the myriad paths or obstacles we encounter every day and that seem to be wrong or out of place because of our mistaken conception of where we are to begin with. No, good maps are not enough to get us home. We also need that divine revelation, that golden key that whispers or states or even screams "You are here!" and points our gaze unmistakably to that place where the map intersects and corresponds with our mortal circumstances. It is this kind of celestial global positioning that changes the gospel from a mass of likely sounding theological assertions into a priceless map of the universe, a treasure map of real places with real treasure at its end.

Kim Nelson's new book, *If God Loves Me, Why This?* is not concerned so much with mapping out the universe as it is with providing the reader with those priceless keys by which we understand our experiences; it tells us, "You are here." Continuing at times in the spirit of his previous book, *The Stillwater Buckskin,* Nelson points out many of the signposts located at the crossroads of human experience. For example, Nelson's discussion of the concept of "fair market value" is typical of how he moves from the theoretical representation of the map to the individual application of the signpost "You are here." Most economists would agree that in the real world fair market value, as opposed to other methods of assigning value, measures only what a buyer is actually willing to pay. However, it follows that if God was willing to sacrifice his Only Begotten Son for each human individual, and if the Son was willing to pay an infinite price in redeeming each of us from the Fall, then the fair market value of each individual, viewed from the perspective of the Father and the Son, must be infinite: "You are here."

Another such signpost is provided by the efforts of the great Adversary to tempt and to destroy us. While it is true that the Enemy has an advantage in this fallen state we now endure, and while it may be true that he is much more clever than we are, how unimportant can we be in the grand scheme of things if this same Adversary seeks at every turn to experience the crumbs of our mortality in stolen, vicarious moments and would pay any price to destroy us? "You are here!" Moreover, it is only through our individual failure in mortality that Satan can justify himself for his rebellion in the premortal world. He needs failed human beings to justify his choices and to give meaning to everything he has lost.

While most of Christianity, following the language of the New Testament, describes God in some way as "the Father," the signpost significance of a term is that the mortal experience of parenthood is a valid way of understanding, not God's importance to us, but rather our importance to God. Yes, the Father is important to his dependent children. But even more important, more dear, more beloved, are the children to their Father. The boundless love of human parents for their offspring is an analogy and a model for understanding God's infinite love for us. The father of the prodigal in the parable really did still love his wayward son!

"You are here!" This is your individual place in the infinite heart of the great, eternal God! It also follows that the greatest blasphemy against God the Father is to be a father who abuses, a father who by his actions makes fatherhood an abomination and makes the Father a monster to be hated or feared. Indeed, it would be better for such to be drowned in the depths of the sea.

I first met Kim Nelson several years ago, and I have since had the opportunity of observing him at work in a professional setting and have discussed his unique counseling abilities with more than one of his clients and patients. To my great benefit, Kim has since that time continued to be one of my closest and most faithful friends. It gives me considerable personal pleasure as well as professional satisfaction to introduce *If God Loves Me, Why This?* which I find to be filled with many of the same counseling methods and spiritual insights Kim has employed with such success in his professional counseling. This is a book that teaches "you are here."

STEPHEN E. ROBINSON

Acknowledgments

In an effort to acknowledge all those who helped in the many tasks and reviews that have made this project come to life, I know I will forget someone. If you are that person, forgive me. All who helped know how human I am, and another evidence of it won't be too surprising.

Thanks to my brothers and sisters in the gospel, who have contributed insights and thoughtful understanding: Don Pugh, David Westra, Mark Middlesworth, Jim Pugh, Larry Watts, Cary and Jeanne Wasden, April and Gary Folkman, Michael and Lynne McLean, Susan and Kevin Pinegar, Laurel Johnson, Debbie Leavitt, Wendy Brinton, Rachel Johnson, and Linda Mahlum.

Thanks to Hollie and John Hansen for interrupting very busy lives to review the final drafts and make suggestions under tight time constraints. Their input was very valuable.

Steve and Janet Robinson are the best of friends and

have given help without reservation. Steve's offer to write a foreword is an example of that friendship and support. I am grateful.

Thanks to Chanda Hair for hours of transcription and review; her talents and commitment were invaluable.

Thanks to Chris Schoebinger, Laurel Christensen, Shauna Gibby, Laurie Cook, Lisa Mangum, and the rest of the team at Deseret Book and Time Out for Women for their support and encouragement. Finally, a special thanks to Jay Parry for a masterful editing job.

The Great Question

Over the years in my experiences as a teacher, a bishop, a friend, a father, a brother, and a counselor, I have heard roughly the same disturbing question asked hundreds— maybe even thousands—of times. It is most often asked by a person who is experiencing some real pain, and it comes in various iterations:

- If God really loves me, why did he put me in a place that hurts so badly?

- If God knows and values me, why did he send me to a place that is so lonely?

- If God really wants me to be happy, why did he put me in a place where I don't have the right skills to be successful?

This is the great question: "If God really loves me, then why . . . " We then fill in the rest of the question with our particular hurts.

How we respond to that question or any of its derivations can, if we aren't careful, lead to some inaccurate conclusion jumping. Even if we start with the accurate belief—"He knows everything, he is in charge of everything, he knew what would happen, and he put me here anyway"—we could end up with some faulty conclusions that might sound like this:

- I must not be very valuable to him.
- I must not be worthy of good blessings.
- He must want me to hurt or fail.
- He must think I need this mess.
- I must have done something to disqualify myself from his love. (Sometimes we even believe ourselves to be disqualified from our Father's love based on poor premortal performance.)

It is a terrible and unnecessary burden to believe that we are living our lives without the support of a loving Father in Heaven. In order to lay that burden down, we must come to know Him. We must remember who we are and what our relationship to God is. We need a clear understanding of four things to make some hopeful sense out of the potentially painful puzzle of mortality.

First, we need to have a clearer picture of how and why we came to earth. Understanding the role we played in this process and getting a vision of the great plan of happiness will help us come to feel confident in the support of heaven.

Second, we need to better understand the nature of God's parental affection for us. Evidences of his love and devotion are all around us. When we recognize and feel that concern, we gain perspective and a sense of our eternal worth.

Third, we must realize the level of the adversary's commitment to keep us from these truths. Satan is the father of all lies. His plan for us is in direct opposition to the Father's great plan of happiness. All the powers and sophistication at his control are being brought to bear to keep us from feeling God's love for and confidence in us.

Fourth, we need to know what we can do to get the most out of this earthly test as we learn and grow. How do we keep from being overcome by the pain that leads us to ask the great question in the first place? How can we learn to see and feel the evidences of God's love and support in our lives? How do we know how we are doing? Is it enough?

Can we receive answers to these questions? Can we grow in the confidence that comes from knowing we have the support of a loving and benevolent Father in Heaven? Of course we can. The prophets through the ages have recognized our need to come to know the nature of God. The value of feeling his confidence in us as we struggle with the tough tests of life cannot be overstated. Modern prophets of God have clearly taught how important we are to him:

"It is the grand truth that in all that Jesus came to say and do, including and especially in His atoning suffering and sacrifice, He was showing us who and what God our Eternal Father is like, how completely devoted He is to His children in every age and nation. In word and in deed Jesus was trying to reveal and make personal to us the true nature of His Father, our Father in Heaven" (Jeffrey R. Holland, "The Grandeur of God," *Ensign,* November 2003, 70).

"God has no distracting hobbies off somewhere in the universe. We are at the very center of His concerns and purposes" (Neal A. Maxwell, "How Choice a Seer!" *Ensign,* November 2003, 100).

We came here to learn to be like our Father, and it is through that process that we can not only find answers to the great question but go on to experience the most that life has to offer.

Part 1

What We Need to Know

CHAPTER 1

Why and How We Came to Earth

One of the most fundamental and significant events of our preearthly existence was what we often call the war in heaven. It was, in fact, the struggle over whether or not we should be trusted to make an informed choice about our mortality. We knew before we came what was at stake and how difficult this earthly place would be. We who supported God's plan decided that our loving Father knew what was best. We let him know with our individual affirmation of his plan that we were willing to come here and learn to be like him. We weighed risk and reward and decided with Father.

Satan wants us to believe that God forced us to come to earth because He enjoys our suffering. He wants us to feel that our Father believes pain is the only way we can learn. He invites us daily to question our Father's love by asking things like: "If God is so powerful, why does he let children die? Why does God allow wars? Why does he not temper the winds and the waves and prevent natural disasters?"

Satan wants us to feel the heavenly equivalent of the rebellious teenage angst that many earthly parents are so familiar with. Haven't most of us parents experienced accusations from our struggling children that we somehow enjoy their pain, even though we just want the best for them? The adversary wants us to feel as if God is shoving His plan down our throats, and we just shouldn't take it. At the very least we should be angry at the Lord and blame him for all our troubles and pain.

Many believe Satan's lie, even though our earthly parental experience teaches exactly the opposite. What really happened makes far more sense.

I believe that in our premortal life, God, presenting what would perhaps be the eternal equivalent of a family home evening lesson, took us all up to a very high place, as he has done with many of the prophets to give them perspective. I can picture him saying: "Here it is, beginning to end. Here's the preearthly existence, where we are now. Here's the earthly trial or test. Here is the eternity that will follow, and here is what is possible for all of you." He showed us and then declared, "I want you to have all that I have."

This was our introduction to God's plan of happiness. When we saw it, we were overcome at the chance of becoming like our Father. But he knew we needed to understand why the test of earth was necessary.

"Here's the challenge," Father may have explained. "You've come this far and learned a lot, but you can't go any further without understanding for yourselves the real difference between good and evil. You must learn by experiencing and feeling the consequences of sin and obedience. That requires that I do not intervene to soften the impact of your choices—or the harmful effect that the choices of others would have upon you.

"For example, if somebody were to choose to hurt you and I didn't allow it, I would be getting in the way of the natural consequence of that person's choice. I would also be eliminating your opportunity to respond to it. If you are really going to have choice and learn from your decisions, you must experience the impact of both negative and positive. For that to happen, I have to get out of the picture. So here's the plan. I propose that you go to earth and experience the natural consequences of choices."

After we thought about it, we must have said, "I make really good choices; it seems like a good plan to me."

Surely our Father reminded us that, as we had seen from our view of earth and from our interaction with our spirit siblings, not everyone would make good choices. Inevitably the fact that some would choose evil would be painful. In many cases, those hurt most would be innocent of wrongdoing.

We realized that the choices of others could be big trouble for us even if we personally made the best use of our agency. We realized that mortal life was going to be really tough. We also came to understand that without that risk, we wouldn't have the reward. We couldn't learn all we needed to without having firsthand experience. So from that high place we took another look. We looked at where we were, where we had always been, what the test would be, and what was at stake.

My guess is that about this time we asked Father if he really thought we could make it. It is the same question our children ask before every big challenge in their lives. He assured us that we could succeed and reminded us of who we were.

During this process, a very powerful and persuasive brother of ours proposed a different plan. He told Father that we could never be trusted to make good choices and would be lost. He suggested that his would be a better idea. The scripture tells us he rebelled against God and sought to destroy the agency of man (Moses 4:3). He would force each of us to behave the way he thought we should, and none would be lost. Unfortunately, no one would grow, either. The obvious difficulty of the test and the smooth persuasiveness of our brother was a powerful opposition to God's proposal and His confidence in us. The fear was so great that a third of the host of heaven followed Lucifer and his plan. They were cast out. And the heavens wept.

Lifted by the confident support of our Father, we made an informed decision to follow the plan. Not only did we decide to participate, but we shouted for joy at the opportunity.

Even though I am encouraged by knowing that God believes I can make it, life can be really hard. It is a little difficult for me to believe some mornings, as I crawl from the relative peace of my bed to face the world again, that I stood up and shouted for joy because of the opportunity to come down here and feel like this.

But here we are, by our own free will and choice, in a place where we are tested every step of the way. As a general rule God doesn't intervene in our choices as we grow and learn. This earthly existence is the test.

We have been put in a fallen place, a mortal place, separate from our immortal Father and our memory of him. It is a place where we physically suffer and die. Consequently, death and the physical pain of mortality, accidents, and illness get added to the consequences of all our choices. So it's not just people's choices that make earth life so difficult, it's also our fallen, mortal, earthly state.

We are in a tough spot. However, we came here knowing that this place and our response to its challenges could make an unlimited eternity of joy possible for us. We chose, with the confidence and support of an all-knowing and loving Father, to come here and learn.

What if our options are limited by the decisions others make? What if our physical condition keeps us from having meaningful life choices? Then the mercy of a loving Father's plan is our hope. The Atonement provides the final leveling of all our obstacles. Our acceptance of the Savior's atoning sacrifice brings us home. We are evaluated on our circumstances and the choices we would have made if we had been free to make them.

It seems impossible to evaluate fairly all the circumstances that affect a person's choices. It would take almost infinite capacity and understanding to take all the variables of a person's life and circumstances into account. Yet that is what is required in any fair and merciful judgment.

We know that God will not allow our agency to be taken from us. So there is a way to provide for those who have been robbed of some of their life choices. *He* is the way, the truth, and the life. The gatekeeper is the Holy One of Israel, and he employeth no servant there (2 Nephi 9:41). That is the key to the whole plan of happiness and the reason joy is within our grasp regardless of what mortality holds for us.

When we truly understand why we came to earth, and that we chose to do so, the answer to the great question, "If God loves me, why this?" becomes much easier to find!

Chapter 2

God's Parental Affection

I believe one of the reasons God included families in this earthly test was to help us understand how much he loves us and our brothers and sisters. I think he wants us to become more like him in this way—he wants us to learn to choose to love ourselves and others in spite of less-than-perfect performance. To paraphrase my friend Stephen Robinson, God doesn't love us because we are particularly lovable. He loves us because he is God, he is our Father, and he has chosen to love us.

Almost all of us have had the opportunity to fall in love with a baby or two in our lives. If you are a mother, how long did it take for you to love your baby after she was born? I ask this question a lot, and the answer I get most often is, "I loved her before she was born." How is it possible that we could love our children before they are born?

What did that baby do to earn your love? What product did the child produce? What did the baby do to earn her food or lodging, let alone your affection and devotion?

Babies are kind of little, bald, toothless, noise machines in the beginning—and we love them anyway. If our little ones don't have to earn our love, why is it we think we have to earn parental love from our Father in Heaven? Why do we have to qualify? Can't he just love us because we are his children?

We love in this way all the time. We give our children our tender affection without even thinking about it. We love our dear friends and family easily. We do this and then disqualify God from that same favorable disposition of the heart when it comes to loving us. We disqualify him with our self-doubt and lack of trust. We disqualify him even after he tells us over and over that he loves us and wants to bless us. We disqualify him even after he blesses us with all we have. The question that derails us is usually a simple one: "How could *He* love *me?*" We should stop beating ourselves up long enough to listen to the answer after asking the question.

He says, "If ye then, being evil, know how to give good gifts unto your children, how much more shall your Father which is in heaven give good things to them that ask him?" (Luke 11:13). He asks, "If a son shall ask bread of any of you that is a father, will he give him a stone? or if he ask a fish, will he for a fish give him a serpent?" (Luke 11:11).

It makes perfect sense to me, especially after observing my own actions as a parent, that we don't have to earn God's parental love. At times he is more pleased with our choices than at other times, just as we are pleased with or dismayed at our own children's choices. But he always loves us, just as we always love them. Some of us, because of our experiences with imperfect people, feel that when we are not making perfect choices God does not love us. We confuse our lack of worthiness and our guilt about it with his willingness to love us. We don't accept his parental affection.

Let's test this theory of his affection for us with our experience. How do we feel about our children when they are less than perfect? Have you ever had a child make a mistake? When he made a mistake or was in a place you wouldn't be, did you love him? Did his choice disqualify him from your concern or affection?

And yet, don't we sometimes imagine that our Heavenly Father reacts to us in a negative way? Have you ever said to yourself, "If I make bad choices, God leaves me"? Don't we think, "If I'm not having the Spirit with me all the time, if I'm not in the temple, if I don't get my visiting teaching done, God doesn't love me"? We often feel that way in spite of the fact that our own parental experience is exactly the opposite!

This earthly experience provides us with an opportunity to become more like our Father in Heaven. Even though a veil has been placed between us and our preearthly life, the individual characteristics we developed there and the influence of our Heavenly Father are still with us. By observing our predispositions here, we come to know more about our Father in Heaven.

Our experiences here teach us how easily we feel charity for our loved ones, no matter what their folly. We need only pay attention to those feelings to identify how our Father in Heaven feels toward us. He loves us and is interested in us in spite of our earthly foolishness and imperfection. He is a concerned and willing parent. As we experience how our concern and support lift others, we can see how Father's affection might lift us if we allow it to.

Our predisposition to care is a reflection of our spiritual heritage—our heavenly genes, if you will. Here is another little test to see how our earthly experience might give us celestial insight.

THE PARABLE OF THE LOST GIRL

If you were to come upon a little girl lost in the store, say a five-year-old who had been careless and wandered away from her mother, what would your first inclination be?

Would it be to say something like this? "You foolish little girl! If you had listened to your mom you wouldn't be in this fix. I hope being lost and crying helps you understand what a bad little girl you have been. It will be your own fault if bad things happen. I bet this will teach you a thing or two about disobedience."

We can't even imagine such a cruel response. Our first inclination would be to help her. The question is, Why? This little child is a helpless stranger. She is not ours. We have no responsibility for her. It was not our mistake that caused her problem. Why do our hearts go out to her?

Our charitable and loving reaction stems from our natural inclination to be like our Father. It is our response to a family member in need. He would have us take a kind and tender approach and help our little sister to safety. That is the very thing he will do for us when we are lost, if we allow him to.

When our kids struggle, we don't love them any less. Isn't God the same way? I think he is. When our children make mistakes, we want to be close to them, not far away. If that is the case, why do we suppose Father withdraws when we are less than perfect? We are the ones who move away, not him.

I remember one night kneeling by the side of my bed to pray for my daughter. I was in tears, frustrated that her choices were so foolish and dangerous. She was having a relationship with somebody who was abusive and disrespectful. I could see where it was going and yet had no influence to stop it.

I remember thinking as I was praying, *This just isn't fair. I am suffering for her choices. She knows better. I am suffering for her sins.* Then a garden near Jerusalem came clearly into my mind. I pictured the Savior suffering for my sins. I realized how benevolent my Father was to offer me the opportunity to feel in some very small way what he and Jesus felt. Being a father gave me a chance to learn how much the Savior loved me. It gave me a glimpse of my Father in Heaven's heart. Being a parent helped me learn that one of the reasons Jesus felt that pain is because he loves us so much. I came to understand that he and Father love us that much in spite of our choices, not because of them.

I have since that night had the experience of watching that daughter make much better choices. It is a wonderful blessing to see her choose more wisely. I have asked myself if I could help my Father in Heaven feel that good. Is it possible that he loves me so much that my good choices could have a positive impact on how he feels?

The answer is yes. He reminds us over and over in the scriptures and in the direction we receive from living prophets that he loves us and cares how we are doing. The thought of that encouraging Father inspires me to try again. I know from my experience as a father how it feels to have a child who keeps trying.

I just think we need to include ourselves in God's family and know that we can be loved in spite of our behavior. When we do that, we understand the true affection of a perfect parent. That understanding opens the door for us to come home to such a Father even after the inevitable mistakes we make. That understanding invites us to leave our door open for our children to do the same.

Another experience familiar to most of us helps explain our Father's love for us and his desire to help us through the challenges of mortality.

THE PARABLE OF THE TRAINING WHEELS

You can probably remember learning to ride a bicycle. I remember how important it was for me. It was that first big step to mobility, the promise of freedom. I could go places that had been out of the question before.

I have observed the process of learning to ride a bike many times over the years—I have even been the teacher a time or two—and I believe that there is a parable of our Heavenly Father's love in this process. Let's walk through it together.

We go to our Father and say, "I want to be able to keep up with the big kids. They can all ride two-wheelers, and I don't know how." Our Father knows us, and he understands the process of learning to ride a bike. This perspective lets him see things we can't. He looks at us and thinks, *You're going to fall; it's going to hurt.* But he loves us and has confidence in us. He knows how badly we want to grow up. So he proposes that we start by getting a bike with training wheels on it. For a while that is great. But when we start riding around with the big kids, what do we discover about our training wheels? They limit us. We really can't keep up. We realize we are really not where we want to be. Our progression is stopped until the training wheels are taken off.

Our loving Father sees our frustration. He loves us. He knows the thoughts have crossed our minds that we can't keep up and will never be able to. He knows we have been prepared and are capable of success. He also knows there is a price to be paid for that success. So because he loves us, because he has confidence and faith in us, he takes off the training wheels and in so doing removes the protection against falling. This is very significant in our earthly lives, because after the protection is removed we will all suffer the effects of the Fall.

God loves us and has the confidence in us to know that eventually we will be able to ride our bikes. Once the decision has been made, he becomes our greatest cheerleader. His belief in us gives us courage. Like any good parent, he wants us to learn in the safest possible way, so we go to the flattest, softest place that can be found, and the great moment arrives. We put on the pads and the helmet and get a final hug of encouragement.

He sets us on the bike and holds onto the seat and gives a gentle push. He does this knowing full well we are going to fall, and it will hurt. And we do, and it does. But when we fall, he doesn't stand back and say, "See, I told you that you were going to fall. If only you had prepared better or been content or . . . "

Every parent knows there is no life without risk. But a child's pain is not an I-told-you-so thing, and our Father is not an I-told-you-so Father. As soon as we fall he rushes to us, picks us up in his arms, and says, "Are you okay? Will you be all right? What can I do?" He provides us a comforter, if you will. And when we're calm enough to see that we're not permanently damaged, he begins to rebuild our confidence.

Notice that we don't have to invite him to help us after we fall. He is there. We do have to accept his help, though. He can't comfort us if we don't allow him to. I think we are often confused about this. We think that he is embarrassed at our failure, or that we need to do this on our own. We're afraid that we are weak or that we've failed if we let him help us.

When my child is hurt, for whatever reason, I want to be there. Our Father in Heaven is that same kind of parent, but infinitely more caring, capable, and reliable. No matter what our earthly experience is with those who have taught us, our Heavenly Father can be trusted. He will be there and he will still believe in us.

It is at this point, after we have fallen, that he does the most difficult and parental thing of all. He picks us up and puts us back on the bike. He knows it's the only way we can ride with the big kids. He comforts us and starts us again, as many times as it takes. As long as we are willing, as long as we allow him, he will continue to encourage and teach us.

Are these first little learning falls the last ones we ever take? No! In fact, I don't know about you, but the worst falls I have ever taken have come way after I knew how to ride a bike. The worst falls have come when I felt very capable and exceptionally cool. "What . . . handlebars for *moi?* What kind of a punk do you take me for? In fact, all of you gather around and please observe how masterfully I ride without the use of hands."

I might add here, in spite of good training and plenty of protective paraphernalia available, there are no knee pads or helmets to be found when I'm playing it cool. It has been at these moments, crowd gathered and watching, that my biggest crashes have occurred.

Even at these times, when I have ignored my Father's advice and training and refused the protective gear he provided, he is still the first one at the scene. His first question is still, "Are you okay?" Not "I told you so," not "See what happens when you don't listen," not "I knew you weren't ready," but "Are you okay?"

I respond, "Yeah, I am, but I'm never going to ride a bike ever again." My confidence is shaken, and the enemy is screaming in my ear that success is impossible and that continued effort will just mean more meaningless pain.

Father is there. He holds me briefly and kisses it better if I let him. He lets me rest a moment and then picks me up. All he says is, "Be more careful. I know you can do it!" He lovingly hands me the knee pads and helmet He always carries. He helps me repair my bike, if required. And then He sets me back on the bike, steadies me, and gives me another confident start. He does that for any of his children whenever they fall, whatever the reason.

Even when he knows he doesn't have to hold onto our seat anymore, he runs by us for a while to remind us to be more careful. He wants us to remember he is always there. That knowledge is what gives us the confidence to ride on even the bumpiest roads. That is why he reminds us over and over in the scriptures that he is available. One of my favorites is Doctrine and Covenants 68:6: "Wherefore, be of good cheer, and do not fear, for I the Lord am with you, and will stand by you."

He does all this teaching and caring and supporting, knowing full well we're going to fall again. These falls are the consequences of our poor choices. Foolishness and sin always lead to pain, but no matter how many times we crash, he is the first one there.

GOSPEL EVIDENCES OF GOD'S LOVE

Sometimes it's hard for us to believe our Father in Heaven could be so patient with us over such a long time. Maybe that's because we live with imperfect people who don't always behave in such a consistently loving way. Our parents provide our first model of what Father in Heaven's love is like, and unfortunately, many times, it has been the wrong model of love. As we know, there is most often no malicious intent in the teachings of those who first cared for us. They were just teaching us what they had been taught. But their lack of perfect parenting skills can be a contributing factor in why many believe that Heavenly Father is insensitive, angry, unkind, and malicious. That just isn't the case.

If the true nature and sweet disposition of God are new concepts to us, we can seek evidence in the gospel. One of the best examples of his concern is in the ordinance of confirmation. It comes in those sweet moments when the very purest among us have chosen to do the right thing and have repented in preparation to receive the gift of the Holy Ghost.

In the prayer of confirmation, there are four words that we have been instructed to use: "Receive the Holy Ghost." God wants us to be taught and protected. He wants us to be comforted. He wants us to accept the gift he has prepared for us to provide that teaching, protection, and comfort.

It is interesting to me that these four words are not a commandment to the Holy Ghost. We are not given this blessing in a way that says, "Holy Ghost, come upon this person." Heavenly Father knows that the Holy Ghost is perfectly dependable and obedient. The Holy Ghost knows his assignment and can be trusted. Instead, God reminds us of our opportunity to accept his love and his affection. When we receive the Holy Ghost, if we are aware of and available to the Spirit, he will be there for us.

This blessing is a demonstration that our Father would never miss an opportunity to remind us of his love. He is directing us to receive the priceless and protecting gift he is perfectly willing to give us as a loving Heavenly Father.

FAIR MARKET VALUE

Of course, the gospel principle that illustrates most clearly the love of God for us is the Atonement. If our mortal challenges are making us feel unloved and attacking our sense of self-worth, we may need to stop and consider: How much are we worth in the economy of heaven?

I believe in the notion that God's economy differs from that of the world. For example, I don't think God cares how rich we are as much as he cares how honest we are. Thinking about his love in economic terms can provide some interesting insights. In particular, there is an economic axiom that teaches a huge lesson about our individual worth: The "fair market value" of an item is established by what someone is willing to pay for it.

I remember as a child going to a livestock auction with my dad and not being able to figure out why some horses or some cows cost a lot more than others. People who really knew stock could have told me; they saw the differences with ease.

My dad said that, without a lot of experience, it was often hard to judge what something was worth. The more you knew about what you were buying, the better idea you had of what it was worth. He taught me that the fair market value or the real worth of something was what someone was willing to pay for it. I've relearned that lesson many times over the years in real estate, collectibles, fly rods, and any number of other possessions. Financial value is about what someone is willing to pay.

I don't have to go down that road very far before I realize what the Savior paid for me. He paid for each of us individually, having a perfect knowledge of what he was getting for his investment. He suffered for our individual sins. He gave his life for us. I think that establishes a fair market value in the economy of heaven.

When we are tempted to say, "I'm not worth very much," or, "Gee, why would anybody want me?" we must remember what our fair market value is. We need to remember how that value was determined and who paid the bill. Our value has already been eternally established—and the price is infinite.

Our Talents—His Love

There is positive power in knowing and feeling the love of a benevolent God as our Father in Heaven. When we experience him in this way, the comforts of his true character are more and more available to us. The scriptures are key in revealing his nature to us.

In the New Testament parable of the talents (Matthew 25:14–30), one part of the story stands out in helping us understand the nature of the Master, and it is one I often miss. I don't know how many times I've read the parable of the talents, but most times, I think I see this story as an exercise in quantity. In other words, some servants are worth more than others. Some servants do a better job than others. Some are slothful or unwise, and some are really good. I think that feeds into the whole "who's better, me or thee?" kind of thinking. There's another way to view the parable that may be more productive.

A quote that I really love from Shakespeare provides a meaningful introduction to the parable of the talents: "Our doubts are traitors and make us lose the good we oft might win by fearing to attempt" (*Measure for Measure,* act 1, scene 4). When we doubt ourselves, we become paralyzed with the fear that "no matter what I do, I'm not good enough, I don't qualify, I'm not as good as . . . " and endless other arguments that stop us before we start. Isn't that essentially what happened to the third servant in the parable? Let's look:

"The kingdom of heaven is as a man travelling into a far country, who called his own servants, and delivered unto them his goods. And unto one he gave five talents, to another two, and to another one; to every man according to his several ability; and straightway took his journey" (vv. 14–15).

In essence, the master left some of his resources in the hands of his servants and said, "Do with these what you can." He gave different amounts to different servants.

Now, don't think it is an accident that these resources are called "talents." These are the things God gives us—call them talents or skills or abilities or understanding or learning or wisdom, it does not matter. After we are separated from our master for a while, a very interesting thing happens. He comes home and asks for a "reckoning."

"And so he that had received five talents came and brought other five talents, saying, Lord, thou deliveredst unto me five talents: behold, I have gained beside them five talents more. His lord said unto him, Well done, thou good and faithful servant: thou hast been faithful over a few things, I will make thee ruler over many things: enter thou into the joy of thy lord. He also that had received two talents came and said, Lord, thou deliveredst unto me two talents: behold, I have gained two other talents beside them. His lord said unto him, Well done, good and faithful servant; thou hast been faithful over a few things, I will make thee ruler over many things: enter thou into the joy of thy lord" (vv. 20–23).

Now, here is the important thing to notice: The master's recognition and satisfaction were not a question of magnitude, because the servant with five talents and the one with two talents got the same reward. God doesn't need our money. God wants us to improve upon what he has given us.

On the other hand we see the impact of fear and inaction: "Then he which had received the one talent came and said, Lord, I knew thee that thou art an hard man, reaping where thou hast not sown, and gathering where thou hast not strawed: and I was afraid, and went and hid thy talent in the earth: lo, there thou hast that is thine" (vv. 24–25).

Now, who was he afraid of? His assumption was that God was a hard man, and if he didn't do well—or, as we often assume, perfectly—God was going to be angry with him and perhaps even punish him. The fear of a God who was not benevolent and not kind led the third servant to bury his effort and hide his talent and go in the completely wrong direction.

The same is true in our lives. That is why the adversary does not want us to know our Father's heart. When we fear God, believing he is unloving or unkind, it causes us to fear to attempt the greatness that we could. We are afraid that if we can't do everything he wants us to do, or if we can't do what he wants us to do perfectly, or if we're not as good as Sister Jones or Brother Joseph, then God is somehow going to punish us. That's not the case. The punishments demanded by the law of justice are for the unrepentant, those who harden their hearts against accepting the gift of the Atonement. We can always expect mercy if we're striving to repent and keep our hearts right (see Alma 12:33–34).

We need to remember what we are taught by Moroni, that God's spiritual gifts are given "unto every man severally, according as he [God] will" (Moroni 10:17). So we know we have talents, and we know he gave them to us. He didn't give me Sister Jones's talents; he gave me mine. The question therefore can't be, "Is God pleased with my talents?" He gave us the talents we have. The question must be, "Is he pleased with how I am applying and developing the talents he gave me?"

Does the thought that God expects perfection or demands we do well compared to others make sense given our parental or life experience? If you have a little daughter who is five and another who is eleven, do you expect the same things from them? No. You expect performance commensurate with their spiritual, emotional, and chronological age. If you have a son who has a musical gift and another who is a gifted athlete, do you expect the same performance from each?

The same is true of our Heavenly Father. He is not going to expect everybody to produce the same results, because we are all at different points in our progression, with different talents.

If you see that little girl doing her very best, is there ever a time you are not going to praise her and love her, even if the outcome isn't great? This question should make it clear that outcome is not the only important thing. If the servant in the parable had at least tried to do something with his one talent, don't you think the Lord would have accepted his efforts?

Consider this further example: What do you have hanging on your refrigerator? If you're a young parent, or a proud aunt, uncle, or grandparent, chances are that you have a display of your children's artwork. What does it look like? Why did you hang it up if it is just scribbles? Why did you hang it up if it is just stick figures? Why did you hang it up if it says "I love you mommy" and the *Y* is sort of like an *R?* Because what is important is not the outcome of the project, it's the intent of the artist. It is the affection of the audience.

To our loving Father in Heaven, what we make of our lives is art, based on the condition and intent of our hearts. In his eyes, our opportunity plus our best effort is a masterpiece.

Remember, then, that God is truly our Father. His love for us is mirrored in our own instincts to love our children and the people we come in contact with in this life. He is there when we fall to pick us up and give us confidence to try again. Our value to him is infinite. His only desire is that we use our talents to the best of our ability.

Understanding the true nature of God as a loving, benevolent parent is crucial when situations arise that cause us to ask the great question, "If God loves me, why this?"

Chapter 3

Satan's Lies

*W*hy is it so difficult to accept the truths that we *chose* to come to mortality and that our Father in Heaven is a loving ally in our experience here? I believe one reason is that Satan works overtime to keep us from seeing those facts. His objectives are in direct opposition to the Father's plan of happiness, for "he seeketh that all men might be miserable like unto himself" (2 Nephi 2:27).

Two Models of Love

There are two models of love in the world: God's model and the adversary's. God's model sounds like this: "Because I love you, I will allow you to bless your life and lives of others with your choices."

Of course, it is only reasonable that the opposite is also true: We can hurt others and ourselves with our choices. However, our Father's plan emphasizes the potential inherent in the positive application of our agency. Whether we make good or bad choices, the fundamental starting point in Heavenly Father's model is unchanged. His plan always begins: "Because God loves me . . . " His unwavering affection for and devotion to his children underscore everything about his plan. It is about us. God's plan is always an invitation for us to become more like him. He is our eternal and perfect parent. He wants us to be happy and healthy.

The gift of agency in Father's plan provides the most perfect earthly opportunity possible for us to be healthy and happy if we choose to learn and grow. It is a simple process. (Remember, *simple* means "not complicated"; *easy* means "not difficult." The correct application of agency may not be easy, but it is fundamentally simple.)

If I make a choice that turns out well, I try to do it again. If somebody does something positive and I am blessed by it, I can see the benefit of that and try to have it happen more often. I may emulate that person or seek to be with him or her more frequently. Positive relationships are built on this divine reciprocity and example.

On the other hand, if I do something that does not go well or am affected by someone in a negative way, I try to avoid those things in the future. Agency gives us the opportunity to learn how to respond in the best possible way to whatever we face, good or bad.

In opposition to this model is the adversary's model of

love. It sounds like this: "If you do what I want or what I tell you to do, then I'll love you. If you earn it, you will be loved." And that actually sounds pretty good, because it seems that if we behave in the way we are told, we will automatically be loved. He provides the picture, and we just connect the dots.

But you know what? There is a reason Satan is called the father of all lies: *He lies.* He will never love us. His intention is never in our best interest.

The basic promise of love in the adversary's plan sets us up for disappointment. He promises us something he will never deliver. In reality, Satan's plan works like this: "Even if you do what I tell you, I'll make sure the bar is raised every time you almost feel good enough. I will make sure the promised satisfaction will be close but always just out of reach. No matter what you do, it will never be enough to satisfy Father." In fact, Satan never wants us to feel good about anything.

It's Satan's plan we see all around us in the world every day. It is the hellish scramble for recognition, power, and gratification that the world says is the key to our satisfaction. In truth, Satan's promise is an empty one. We can never be rich enough, we can never be thin enough, and we can never be young or powerful enough to feel good enough. The adversary makes sure we never quite qualify.

Unfortunately, many of us have been taught and believe the promise of the world. We have been taught that all love must be earned, that we must look or act or be a certain way in order to have value. We see the ads for what or how we must be every day, but the harder we run toward those things, the farther away they get. Like a mirage in the desert, the refreshing pool looks to be just ahead, but it is never what it seems. Our thirst is never quenched by the adversary.

Let's see how we might experience each model of love. Let's imagine goofing up under each plan and follow the process where it takes us.

If we fall short or make a mistake, here's how it sounds if we assume God's plan: "Oh, my gosh, I have made a mistake. Luckily, Heavenly Father loves me. He put a plan together for my happiness that reflects his love for me. He knew I would not be perfect. The Savior has made meaningful repentance possible. I'm going to get up and try again. I know I can do better. I can learn from this. All is not lost."

The most basic building block of this plan is the affection of our Father. He knew we would not be perfect, but he knew we could learn, and he wants us to. He is there to help us try again.

Now, if we goof up under the adversary's plan, it sounds like this: "Oh, my gosh, I have made a mistake. I failed to qualify for love again. I am so worthless. I'll never make it. I can't do it. I'm just not good enough. I don't have what it takes to be successful. I don't have the right family or education to make it anyway—why even try? The world belongs to the perfect people, and I'm not one of them."

The most basic building block of Satan's plan is the promise that we will be loved if we produce as required. Here love is not given, it is earned—purchased with our perfect performance. Please note that since no one is going to perform perfectly, this plan guarantees that no one can ever earn love.

We need to remember that the disappointment we feel because of our poor responses is not necessarily a bad thing. But there is a huge difference between what Elder Neal A. Maxwell so beautifully described as "divine discontent" and the feeling that our choice has disqualified us from the powerful affection of God. Divine discontent moves us to improve. It helps us recognize our desire to be a better son or daughter of our loving Father. The guilt or shame of the adversary's plan, on the other hand, just leads us to despair.

Unfortunately, it is not always easy to tell the two plans apart even when we are aware of them. For example, my father could say to me, "Kim, wouldn't you really rather be a doctor?" That could mean, "I know the intent of your heart. I know what your goals are. You have always wanted to be a doctor. You can do anything you want. I love you to death. I know you can do it, and I support you in your dream."

Or it could mean, "Boy, I sure would like to tell all my friends my son is a doctor. If you become a doctor, I will really love you."

The intent of the heart of the person speaking is the only way to tell which model of love you're getting. Does the person you are interacting with have your best interest at heart, or his own?

Many times it is hard to know the intent of someone's heart, even with the people we know the best. But there is one Being whose heart we can always know. I can guarantee, when Heavenly Father deals with us, it is always about us. He always puts our well-being first. On the other hand, when Satan deals with us, it is always about him.

Heavenly Father wants our experience and choices to bring out the best in us. When he interacts with us, it is always about teaching us something or helping us grow. He wants us to learn something that we can use to bless ourselves or others or to avoid needless hurt or pain in the future. When Satan interacts with us, he wants us to experience pain and suffering. He wants us to fail. He wants to prove he was right in his evaluation of us. He wants to prove we are not worthy of the trust God has given us.

Satan would have us believe that God will love us only if we earn it, that our perfect or near-perfect performance is required before God will love us. That is a lie!

TEMPTATIONS AND FLY FISHING

One of the primary ways Satan lies to us is to promise us great pleasure or rewards for behaving in ways contrary to our Father's plan for us. The simple word for that tactic is *temptation*. Understanding how temptation works can give us a leg up on resisting this lie of the adversary.

I love to fly fish and can see many parallels between fly fishing and the tempting we receive from the adversary. The common ground is deception and vulnerability. Let's talk about fishing, and let's talk about tempting.

To catch fish, here is what you need to know. You need to know what fish like and what they need. You need to know where they like to be. You need to know what makes them angry, when and how they reproduce, and where they live. You need to understand what makes them feel safe. When you understand those things, you will know when and where they are most vulnerable.

When the adversary is tempting us, he needs the same information. After many centuries of knowing and observing us, he knows what we like and what we need. He knows where we like to go. He knows what makes us angry, when and how we reproduce, and where we live. He understands what makes us feel safe and overconfident. He has done his homework and understands when and where we are the most vulnerable. He has studied and practiced for millennia.

When I'm fly fishing, I need a good fly rod, an

accurate cast, and a good line that can't be seen. The hook has to be sharp and not too obvious, so as not to spook the fish. I need a good selection of artificial flies and good clippers because I have to change the flies often; if one is not working, I'll try another one. Finally, I need patience. I understand that there will be a time when every fish will bite.

Let's talk about the gear Satan uses. He has a good presentation and always casts accurately. He has a great line. It always sounds fun, powerful, or important. He also makes sure his hooks are well hidden. His selection of artificial rewards is huge. Everything looks like something it isn't. He has lots of helpers, and they change the enticement often. He has almost infinite patience; he knows us and all our habits. He knows what has the best chance to hook us.

With fish, some species are harder to catch than others. That challenge makes them the most fun to try to catch. Ultimately, they can all be fooled by something. Some will fight and get away; the species that don't stop fighting are the ones that get away the most often.

Satan expects that some of us will be harder to catch than others, but he knows we can all be fooled by something. He will keep trying.

The adversary is the father of all lies. He never gives us anything without a hook in it and never gives us anything of real, eternal value. Unlike most fly fishermen, Satan never practices catch and release. His objective, should he catch us, is to pull us from the safety of our homes and destroy us. His purpose is to prove our Father was wrong to believe in us, and the way for him to do that is to destroy us. He is committed to do whatever it takes to do just that.

What can we do? If we do get hooked by the adversary, we need to fight and never stop fighting until we get away. We need to shun his lies and turn our faces to the truth of our Father's plan. We need to embrace the Spirit and learn with practice to better recognize the real thing when we see it.

BELIEVING LIES

When we act as if something were true when it is not, we create problems and frustrations that might be avoided. These lies we have come to believe create blind spots in our vision of life. One of the biggest and most successful lies that the adversary uses to discourage us is a belief that our failure is inevitable. This lie might come disguised in any number of ways. Whatever the disguise, it is designed to keep us from feeling successful and worthy. It is this kind of thinking that makes us blind to our own possibilities. We must find and remove these blind spots. For example:

I don't come from the right family.
I have already sinned so much I can't come back.

I am the black sheep of the family.
I was never good at school; I guess I'm just dumb.
I don't have the right connections.
I married the wrong guy; I will never be happy.

Many of our blind spots are evident to those around us. How often have you seen the potential in someone you love and been amazed that they couldn't see it? We all have some of this faulty thinking. The reason we can't see the flawed thinking in ourselves is that we have believed the lie for so long it hasn't crossed our minds not to accept it as true. It is so ingrained that we don't think to question the logic of it.

Here is an extreme illustration that demonstrates how such a blind spot operates. Let's say I believe that a door is open, but really it is closed. I walk toward it, expecting to walk through the open door. Instead I walk into the closed door, and bam! I bloody my nose and fall to the ground. I get up and do it again about forty or fifty more times with the same painful result. Why don't I just open the door? Because it never occurs to me that I should. My fundamental belief is that the door is already open. I don't question that—even though all the evidence and my pain say the door is closed.

Let me share a couple of case studies as examples of what this process looks like in real life.

A guy came into my office and sat down on the couch. He said experience had taught him that counselors didn't know much—but, being open-minded and honoring the request of his wife, he came to me.

He began his story this way: "Every counselor I have talked to has told me that I am lazy and that I don't accept responsibility for my actions. My wife tells me I'm lazy and irresponsible. The same is true of my ex-wife and all my ex-employers. Everybody judges me. The real problem is that nobody understands my talent. They won't take the time to think outside the box."

After an hour of listening to his story and asking a few questions, I came to the same conclusion that everyone else he mentioned had come to. The man was not willing to work. He refused to accept responsibility for his actions—or, in this case, his lack of actions. He asked my opinion, and I shared it with him as frankly and kindly as I could. His response was to point out that his original assessment of counselors had been correct. He left the office and never looked back—or in the mirror at himself.

I had another client come in a few days later. He was a vice president of local software company, a Church leader with a large and active family, and a man I knew well and respected. I thought of him as energetic, successful, and competent.

He seated himself and said, "With my Church calling, my family, and my job, I work sixteen to eighteen hours a day every day." I knew that was true and suspected he might be in my office to talk about depression or anxiety.

But what he said next surprised me. Perhaps this surprise was magnified because of my recent experience with the lazy man I just described. The vice president continued: "I feel lazy all the time. No matter how hard I work or how much money I make, I can't seem to shake the feeling that I am lazy."

As we talked, he told me he knew exactly when he started believing that way about himself. When he was about fifteen years old, living in rural Idaho, his uncle, who was a hero to him, came home from the mission field. He really respected and looked up to this uncle. It was late summer, and they were working on a dairy farm, bucking hay, when his uncle made this offhand remark: "You're kind of a lazy little stinker, aren't you?" Even though he was telling me this at least thirty years later, he remembered the comment exactly. He told me how it had stung him. No matter what he tried, he had never been able to shake that message. He felt lazy all the time.

So, we have one guy who is lazy as sin, with everybody in his life telling him he is, and he won't believe it. He won't believe it in spite of failed marriages and missed employment opportunities. He won't believe it even though these failures could easily be traced to his lazy and blaming habits—if he would just look.

And we have another guy working his brains out and feeling lazy all the time because of what one person told him thirty years before. He feels lazy in spite of substantial evidence in his life of valuable accomplishments. Both those men believed lies that kept them from feeling more happiness and peace in their lives.

We can't always know why we choose to believe what we believe. What we *can* know, though, is that if we believe lies and act as if they are true, it can be real trouble. Generally, when we run into difficulties over and over in the same area of our thinking, there is something there we ought to look at. There is a real chance we are believing something that is not true, or we wouldn't keep having trouble there.

I share the following example with the permission of the person I am describing, although I have not used any names. This is one of the saddest and most wasteful examples of believing a lie that I can imagine. I'd like to preface it by thanking my friend for allowing me to share her experience so someone else might avoid a similar useless hurt.

Several months ago a woman came into my office whom I had known, along with her dear husband, for many years. I asked why she had come in, and tears welled up in her eyes. She said that now that the children were gone, she was going to get a divorce. You could have knocked me over with a feather. I would never have guessed that there was a problem in this marriage. I was speechless. It took a moment for me to recover. When I did, I asked, "Why?"

She explained that she could no longer live with the pressure of not knowing when her husband would cheat on her. She loved him so much, and that made the waiting just too painful.

I was confused. Had there been any evidence of infidelity? No. Were there signs of disinterest? Had they been fighting? No.

"I know your husband," I said. "He adores you. What has he done to make you think he is considering breaking his covenant with you?" She looked at me as if I were just clueless and dropped the lie right into my lap, as if it were almost so obvious it did not even need to be said. Everybody knew it.

"All men cheat on their wives," she said.

It was not stated as a question. It was a fact. She knew the infidelity was coming, and she loved her husband so much that she just couldn't take it. It was better to be divorced than to have to wait, not knowing when the other shoe would drop.

There was not the faintest hint of anything in her face but pain. She believed what she was saying without any question.

"How do you know all men cheat?" I asked. She told me her father and both her grandfathers had been untrue. Her brothers, all four of them, had been unfaithful. Several uncles she knew of had cheated.

Her mother had taken her aside several weeks before

her marriage—her temple marriage—and had told her there was no way for men to avoid it. It was a physical thing. Men had to have more than one woman. These weren't bad men, and some held out longer than others, but in the end it didn't matter. They couldn't help it; it was the way they were made.

"Do you think your husband has cheated on you?" I asked.

"No," she said. Then she looked me square in the eyes and said one of the saddest things I have ever heard: "He just hasn't found the right woman yet."

I sat for a moment and shared her broken heart. Then I took a deep breath and asked, "Do you think President Hinckley cheated on his dear bride?"

"Of course not!" she said without a second's thought.

"I thought you said *all* men cheat. You have known me for more than twenty years. Do I cheat on Lois?"

She paused a long time and thought. It was with a lot of difficulty that she said, "I don't think so."

"I do not," I confirmed. "I love her as much as it looks like I do. I take my temple covenant seriously and try every day to be a better husband. And I am not alone." I then listed several men we both knew and repeated my question, "Do they cheat?"

As incredible as it sounds, this was the first time she had ever looked at that lie seriously. For twenty-five years she had just accepted the inevitability of a cheating husband and the pain that went with that.

Suffice it to say, there won't be a divorce. Once such a lie is discovered for what it is, the evidence of the truth sweeps it away.

We know who encourages such garbage. We know who fathers such damage. So what can be done about these lies and the blind spots they create? Look at the beliefs in your life that foster hopelessness or guilt. List those things that cause you to feel bitter or disqualified from feeling God's love. The truth is always full of hope and light. If that is not what you are seeing, there is a lie in there somewhere. The light will come when that lie is exposed.

BLESSINGS AND LOVE

True or false: "God blesses me because he loves me." True, of course, but Satan has a way of making us reinterpret that belief to mean, "The way I know if God loves me is that he gives me stuff. He gives me what I want." This is the logical bind that comes from believing a lie. It is the adversary's little twist on the divine plan. The father of all lies says: "Let's help the people feel unvalued, unimportant, unloved, and disqualified. Most of the people who feel this way will give up, and those that don't will be miserable in spite of all their efforts. We will do this by telling them that God is in charge of who gets all the toys on earth. He gives his favorites the good stuff, and he gives challenges to the children he doesn't like."

Follow the faulty logic:

Being rich is a blessing.
God blesses those he loves.
Therefore, if I am not rich, he does not love me.

Here's another one:

Being naturally thin is a blessing.
God blesses those he loves.
Therefore, if I am not naturally thin, he does not love me.

Having perfect children or ideal health or any other single object of our desire can be placed on the proof-of-love altar. Anything we want that we don't have is "proof" that God likes someone else better than us.

If we buy these lies, we even turn this logic around and assume that everything we have that someone else doesn't have is proof that God loves us more than them. The bigger the house, the higher on the hill we live, which high school we go to, who we eat lunch with—all these are proofs positive of whom God likes best.

There are at least two problems with accepting these lies. The first is that this approach assumes we know what a blessing is. The second is that we often choose a single indicator of Father's affection. Our having or not having it establishes our chosen blessing as the single proof of whether or not our Father in Heaven loves us.

Oh, how much better off we would be if we just read King Benjamin's address (Mosiah 2–4) and remember that God loves all his children and blesses them. I would even go as far as to suggest that we would be better off to realize that this life is our chance to prove that we are God's friends, that we love and appreciate him, not the other way around.

LETTING GO OF SINS

One of the best ways for us to express our love for our Father in Heaven is to let go of our sins. I've been amazed at how difficult it is for many of us to part with behaviors that are self-destructive. This is difficult even when people openly recognize and admit the destructive nature of the behavior. I've come to recognize two apparent causes of this pattern, and Satan's lies are integral to both.

First, we use our past mistakes to serve as a rationale to keep the door open to further behaviors that might seem pleasant or exciting—in spite of the fact that we know they are also potentially painful and wrong. Satan whispers to us, "You're already soiled, so a little more won't hurt. What if you miss something by repenting too soon?"

Brother Stephen E. Robinson points out: "Individuals who commit the moral and doctrinal error of refusing to do what they could very well do seek to be saved in their sins rather than from their sins. But that can never happen. There is a vast difference between viewing my sins as enemies from which I'm trying with difficulty to escape and viewing my sins as comfortable old friends I'm reluctant to leave behind" (*Believing Christ: The Parable of the Bicycle and Other Good News* [Salt Lake City: Deseret Book, 1992], 86).

When we get beyond the fear that we might miss something, and recognize the good sense of avoiding the lies and pain of the adversary, we are often faced with a second challenge. Satan tries to make us believe that when we repent or try to do better, God will hold us to a new, perfect standard of accountability. This misplaced fear keeps us from trying. In truth, all Heavenly Father wants, no matter where we are in the process, is our best effort and our happiness. Overcoming these two lies of the adversary will help us begin and sustain real change in our lives.

We know the truth, and we know what Satan will do to keep us from believing it. When we turn our backs to the adversary's tactics, our trust in Heavenly Father and his divine plan for us will increase, and we will go forward in the confidence that God will always love us.

Part 2

What We
Can Do

CHAPTER 4

Getting the Most Out of Life

*W*here do we go from here? How do we use what we are learning to get the most out of our earthly experience? How can we better understand our current situation to find peace here and work toward getting home successfully?

To this point, we have looked at how and why we chose to come to this earthly place to be tested and to grow. We have affirmed our choice to follow God's great plan of happiness. We have reexamined the love and confidence our Father in Heaven has for us. We have looked at the intense hatred of the adversary and have become aware of his willingness to do almost anything to bring about our misery and failure.

We have been reminded of the model of love that Father has given us. God's pattern of loving his children affirms our value as his sons and daughters and demonstrates his confidence in us. He has blessed us with agency and encourages us to use it to bless ourselves and others. He wants us to learn from our successes and failures. Most of all, he loves us.

On the other hand, we have seen the adversary's plan. It is a process full of self-serving deceit. He wants us to fail. The adversary needs only to distract us from our objective or confuse us about our location to make us feel lost. To get us to stop trying, he just needs to convince us that our efforts are in vain.

How do we learn and grow while at the same time avoiding as much of the pain of temptation and mortality as we can?

We need to become comfortable with the battle and seek the truth about the power we have to find peace here and to return to our Father successfully. In order to do this, we must learn to behave according to the things we say we believe. We need to be aware of the common physical challenges of this life, so that we will not lose courage when we are assaulted by them. We need to recognize blessings when they come, in whatever form, and be grateful for them. We need to learn to trust others, ourselves, and God. We need to serve and obey. And finally, we need some tests to know how we are doing. Is it working? Are we getting the most we can out of life?

To know where we are going and how we are progressing, we have to be able to assess, accurately and honestly, our current location. Knowing where we are all the time is vital to charting the proper course home. Let me share a story about how a very wise man taught me this principle.

When I was a young married man, a friend asked me a favor. My friend was a very old Navajo medicine man, and we had gotten acquainted when my wife and I moved onto the reservation to live. He and I often talked of the gospel and the challenges of life. Our relationship grew, and I learned a lot from him. He was a spiritual man; he loved life and was always up for an adventure. Although he had traveled extensively as a young man, he had not been far from the reservation in many years. He told me he had heard of a new shopping mall in Albuquerque, New Mexico, and he wanted to see what it looked like. He asked if I would take him to see it.

As I recall, the mall apparently had a huge indoor fountain, and that intrigued him. The idea of an indoor stream was just too much to resist. He said he was not sure his truck would make the trip, and he did not want to leave the reservation without reliable transportation. He thought my car had a better chance of negotiating the distance successfully. I remember thinking that was not so much an endorsement of my car as a confession of how really unreliable his truck was. I think, looking back, that he also wanted to share the trip with me and that after a long winter he had a bit of cabin fever.

So, armed with faith and gas money, we started for the

mall. It was several hundred miles away, and our all-day adventure is one I remember with real fondness. We passed the time talking about the world in general, solving all kinds of problems, as friends do when they take the time to talk. He reminisced about his boyhood, how he was taken to an all-Indian boarding school and received his education. He said that at first he had hated the school but had, over time, appreciated the experience. He had learned to read there, and that gift had been one he had taken advantage of throughout his life. He was a voracious reader and loved to talk about current events and history. He talked about being taught by his father and grandfather in the traditional ways of the Navajo. He told me about his time in the army during World War I. It was a great ride, and I enjoyed his wisdom and insights.

We got to the mall and spent the bulk of the day in and around the city. We shopped, had lunch and dinner, and just generally had a wonderful time. The trip back was uneventful, and we arrived home safely. Just before turning onto the road to his home, I asked what part of the trip was his favorite. I don't know what I expected to hear, but his answer was a real surprise.

"That is easy," he said. "I liked the 'you are here' sign at the mall. The pointing finger was a wonderful thing." As we talked, he described how much he had appreciated the mall map and directory with the red pointing finger labeled "You are here." His next words have stayed with me for thirty years and have proven to be as profound as they are simple:

"It is wonderful to know where you are. Once I knew that, I could go anywhere on that map and return safely. I was not lost."

This little parable has been with me every day since that time. I know if I can keep track of where I am, I can find my way home.

Wouldn't it be nice to know, every day, where we are? I have tried over the years to recognize the "you are here" signs in my life. The global positioning apparatus of prayer, obedience, scripture study, and Spirit of the Holy Ghost help me locate my position. Knowing our Father and recognizing his loving invitation to us to rejoin him have helped me keep my destination in focus.

Chapter 5

Living What We Believe

My wife, Lois, and I both taught early-morning seminary, and both our daughters attended. Our family has
joked over the years that if you were too tired or drifted
off in class and were then called on to answer a question,
you could just say, "Say your prayers, read your scriptures,
and participate in all your meetings." Much of the time
that would be the right answer. In our family we call this
list the "seminary answer."

It doesn't matter where in the Church you teach. If
you ask youth or adults, "What is the right answer to
almost all Sunday school or seminary questions?" they
will generally give a form of those three answers, and
often in the same order.

Why are these "the answers"? Because they really *are*
the answers most of the time. Saying our prayers, reading
our scriptures, and attending our meetings consistently

will help us understand the principles of the gospel and provide us opportunities to apply them. That understanding and application will give us the best possible shot at succeeding and being happy.

A couple of sports analogies help explain why it is so important for us to study the scriptures, say our prayers, and attend our church meetings. In both the football huddle and the basketball time-out, we discover the importance of preparing in advance. Let's look at each.

First, the football huddle. Long before the season begins, football teams practice. They get in shape, learn their playbook, and memorize their assignments from the playbook. They see that everybody has an orchestrated opportunity to contribute in some way to make each play work. The book teaches them specific principles for specific situations.

In a game, there isn't time to sit down with each individual person and tell him what he is going to do on the next play. But if a player has prepared, he can step into the huddle between plays and, in less than twenty seconds, get an assignment and know what he is supposed to do.

A similar kind of preparation is available to us spiritually. For example, our scriptural playbook says, "As [a man] thinketh in his heart, so is he" (Proverbs 23:7). So, in the heat of the game of life, if I find myself thinking something I don't want to think, I change that thought because

I understand the principle. The time to prepare is long before I find myself out on the field in a difficult situation.

Constant prayer is the moment-to-moment huddle with the Spirit to check the play and our assignment. He reminds us of the basic game plan of our lives—the big principles: I want to be with Heavenly Father again in the celestial kingdom. I will keep my temple covenants. I will go; I will do. All those principles are part of our playbook, and the more familiar we become with that book, the easier it is for us to remember what our assignments are in different situations when the game is on the line.

Now let's discuss the example of a basketball time-out. Those who have played know how common it is, especially toward the end of a hotly contested game, to hear the coach say something like this: "All right, we're going to run play number 1." Or he may motion from the sidelines, holding up a certain number of fingers to designate a specific play. Because of the team practices, all the players know what they're going to do. They don't have to draw it up or ask who stands where; they've practiced it a hundred times. Preparation is what gives us the confidence to win.

At the end of a rugged day, I always run my old standby reliable play: prayer. I've done it a thousand times and more. I know it works. I have that dependable play to fall back on at any given time. I practice and practice and practice, and it prepares me. It gives me confidence. With that confidence comes peace in the pressure of the game, peace that I'll know exactly what to do. I'll know who's standing where. I'll know who I can count on, and I'll know to whom I can look for advice and counsel.

Saying our prayers, reading our scriptures, and participating in all our meetings and callings—all those activities prepare us to respond in those times of great stress and pressure in our lives. When seconds count, or when we are tired or drifting and life calls on us to come up with an answer, I would suggest the seminary answer: Say your prayers, read your scriptures, and participate in all your meetings. Chances are, those are the things that will work.

Believing What We Teach

It is one thing to know the seminary answer. It is another thing to believe that it works. Life has a way of presenting us with experiences that really test whether we believe in the principles of the gospel or not. If our behavior would only match more closely our professed beliefs, we would be much happier.

Sometimes our children are our best examples in this regard. I am convinced that we need to have the faith of a little child to recognize the hand of a loving Father in our lives. In the book *The Road Less Traveled,* by M. Scott Peck, there is a whole chapter on how we miss the gift of God's grace by mislabeling his blessings as serendipity or luck. Why is it so difficult to acknowledge his tender care and the fulfillment of his promises to us?

Not long ago, one of the sweetest people in my life passed away. He was my brother-in-law Derrel. Everyone just called him Big D. He had been one of my heroes and one of my favorite people since I was three. He was a big man and incredibly strong. Arthritis had been a serious challenge for him most of his adult life, but in spite of almost constant pain he had kept an easy laugh and a kind and pleasant disposition. He was loved and appreciated as a gentle, good man by everyone who ever knew him.

Western Washington state, near Seattle, where he lived, has a very moist climate, which was not easy on his joints. For many years he wanted to go east of the mountains, where it was dry and his arthritis could get a little better. He wanted to move to the sunshine where he could grow a huge garden. He prepared for retirement and with his wife, my sister Kay, bought a place in Pasco, Washington. The water there is good, and the ground is fertile, and it is a warm and sunny climate. They bought a place with plenty of ground and built a brand-new home.

In the final stages of getting his first garden prepared to grow, Derrel went back to the house one afternoon, sat down in his chair, had a heart attack, and died. It was that fast. His death was devastating for everyone. We had been so excited for him to have his dream. His passing was a tremendous loss to all of us, most of all to Kay.

I have a grandson who at that time was about five years old, a little red-headed boy named Kolby. Kolby is a joy. Kolby is a tender, gentle, good boy, and he loved his uncle Big D. He thought Derrel was the greatest thing in the world. Derrel would talk to him man-to-man, feed him ice cream, and do all kinds of other wonderful things. Kolby's memories of Aunt Kay and Uncle Big D were nothing but good.

About five or six months after Derrel's death, Kay was visiting us and stopped in to see my daughter's family. Kolby came into the room. Kay and he were there alone, and he noticed that she had been crying. He looked at her and said, "Aunt Kay, what's the matter?"

My sister said, "I'm just sad about Uncle Derrel."

Kolby patted her on the hand and looked at her and asked, "Aunt Kay, haven't you heard about the resurrection?"

When she told me that story, she said that of all the comfort she received after her husband's death, that was the sweetest. It was a child's simple understanding and testimony that gave her the most solace.

Kolby had a great sense of loss that his uncle wasn't there, but no fear at all about the hope that lies in the resurrection and the atonement of Jesus Christ. Kolby believed without question that Big D was in heaven waiting and we would all get to see him again.

I taught a CTR 8 class once, and it had to be the greatest teaching time of my life. It was the year the kids in the class were baptized. I have taught seminary, institute, priesthood, and gospel doctrine. I have experienced the joy of sharing the gospel in every one of those environments. But somehow, when it comes to witnessing faith, none of those experiences hold a candle to that CTR class experience for me. I have mentioned this to many people over the years, and it is surprising to me how many have had similar spiritual experiences teaching these children.

I asked a wise friend why he felt this was the case. He reminded me that these kids are ideal students. They are old enough to understand and be accountable, yet young enough to believe without baggage. I like that term a lot. I think when the Lord tells us to become as a little child, one essential thing he is doing is inviting us to believe without baggage.

For example we were given some very specific promises by President Gordon B. Hinckley when he challenged us to read the Book of Mormon by the end of 2005. Many showed great faith and obedience by picking up their books and beginning to read. They didn't question the promises of the prophet but believed without baggage.

Elder Henry B. Eyring used the specific promises of the

prophet and his response to it to teach this principle of faith beautifully in October conference that same year.

In August, you received this promise from President Gordon B. Hinckley if you would read the Book of Mormon through by the end of the year: "Without reservation I promise you that if each of you will observe this simple program, regardless of how many times you previously may have read the Book of Mormon, there will come into your lives and into your homes an added measure of the Spirit of the Lord, a strengthened resolution to walk in obedience to His commandments, and a stronger testimony of the living reality of the Son of God."

That is the very promise of increased faith we need to be spiritually prepared. But if we delayed the start of our obedience to that inspired invitation, the number of pages we had to read each day grew larger. If we then missed reading for even a few days, the chance of failure grew. That's why I chose to read ahead of my daily plan to be sure I will qualify for the promised blessings of the spirit of resolution and testimony of Jesus Christ. When December ends, I will have learned about starting at the moment a command from God comes and being steady in obedience (Eyring, "Spiritual Preparedness: Start Early and Be Steady," *Ensign,* November 2005, 38–39).

I have a favorite scripture that invites us to be just like my grandson or the children in my CTR class: "Be ye therefore followers of God, as dear children; and walk in love, as Christ also hath loved us, and hath given himself for us an offering and a sacrifice to God for a sweet-smelling savour" (Ephesians 5:1–2).

When we teach our children and new investigators the gospel, we are telling the truth. We need to remember that those fundamental principles apply to us as well as to them. We should listen to the gospel we teach.

As a bishop I had the opportunity to fellowship the new husband of a sister in our ward who was dear to me. She had been divorced and now had married a man who was not a member of the Church. In fact, he had been a Lutheran lay pastor as a younger man. He too had been divorced and was wise enough to seek out a worthy mate. He is one of the best men I know.

Here is his story, to the best of my memory. I use it with his permission. He called me on the phone one night and said, "Bishop, could you come over and give me a blessing?" He was going in for some very serious back surgery. I called a friend, and we went over and gave him a blessing. In that blessing, the Lord promised him he would heal. There was a sweet spirit there that evening, and it touched him. He healed up as promised, and we were all grateful for and acknowledged the power of the Lord in that process.

Several months later, he called me on the phone one Sunday evening and said, "Bishop, what do I have to do to qualify to be baptized?"

I said, "Well, that's an interesting question. Why?"

He said, "I've done some reading, and I know the gospel is true. When I received that blessing from Heavenly Father I felt a power I had not experienced before. I know it was the power of the priesthood that healed me. As I said, I've done some studying and I need to know what I have to do to qualify to be a member."

I said, "You have to take the missionary lessons. You've been coming to church, and you would need to have a brief baptismal interview from one of the supervising missionaries."

He said, "The way my travel schedule looks, I'd like to take those lessons on Monday. Could I be baptized on Tuesday or Wednesday?"

I said, "You probably don't want to do it that fast; the missionaries need to teach you several lessons. Not only that, but there are some people who would like to be there to see it happen. Have you spoken to your children?"

"I have," he said, "and they are supportive."

I suggested he would want to invite them and some of his friends as well. He decided that would be a good idea to consider.

He said, "I've read the Book of Mormon and the King James Version of the Bible and the Doctrine and Covenants and Pearl of Great Price and *Jesus the Christ* and *A Marvelous Work and a Wonder*," and he listed several others. Then he said, "I have notes on them all, but that's not really what is important here, is it?"

I said, "No."

He went on, "I have prayed, and God told me it is the true church. I've felt the power of the priesthood and I'm ready to be baptized."

I said, "Well, I'll call the elders and see what we need to do."

So I made one of the most enjoyable telephone calls I have ever made. I reached the elders' answering machine and said, "If you want a baptism, call me back." They called about twenty minutes later, and we set up the first discussion at my house.

It ended up taking about two weeks to get that good brother taught and baptized. He is a giant, and his testimony is a powerful belief in what he was taught by those good missionaries and had confirmed to him by the Holy Ghost. Those teachings, coupled with his ongoing study and the continued promptings of the Spirit, make up his faith.

The reason he is such a great example to me is that he really believes the gospel applies to all of us. He is not afraid to think he is included.

About a year after his baptism, I was going in for surgery, and he called me on the phone. Here is the gist of that funny and powerful experience as I recall it. "Bishop," he said, "I hear you're going to get some surgery."

"Yes, I am."

"I hold the Melchizedek Priesthood and can bless you."

"Yes, you can."

"Would you like me to do that? And when?"

"How about tonight?"

He said, "Will you get someone to help me? Because this is one of those blessings it takes two to do, you know."

I said that I did know that and then asked, "Do you have oil?"

He said, "I have it. I consecrated it myself."

I called my home teacher to assist him in the blessing.

They came and he gave me a blessing, but that is not all. He provided me with a handwritten piece of paper to put by my bed. His notes referenced places in the scriptures and Church history where the blessing of the priesthood had healed people. He told me further that I could count on this because he was a member of the true Church, a holder of the Melchizedek Priesthood, and the blessing he had pronounced by that power was from God.

He then told me the purpose of his note: "I want you to tape this up by your bed, and if you have any questions about what to expect as you heal, just read what's written there."

I had a wonderful recovery, and the whole thing was a great testimony-building experience. He was a wonderful example of believing and applying diligently what he had been taught.

"GREAT FAITH HAS A SHORT SHELF LIFE"

Feeding our spiritual selves every chance we get is the best way to nourish our souls. We need to prepare for life's storms if we want to do better when they come. And we need to keep preparing and keep growing in faith if we are to have what we need in times of trouble.

Elder Henry B. Eyring of the Quorum of the Twelve made a profound observation along these lines in a conference address. He spoke of following President Hinckley's counsel to read the Book of Mormon by the end of the year, and said: "We will then have a choice of what to do after January 1. We can choose to sigh with relief and say to ourselves: 'I have built a great reservoir of faith by starting early and being steady in obedience. I will store it away against the times when I will be tested in storms.' There is a better way to prepare, because great faith has a short shelf life. We could decide to persist in studying the words of Christ in the scriptures and the teachings of living prophets. This is what I will do. I will go back to the Book of Mormon and drink deeply and often. And then I will be grateful for what the prophet's challenge and promise did to teach me how to gain greater faith and maintain it" ("Spiritual Preparedness: Start Early and Be Steady," *Ensign*, November 2005, 39).

His wise counsel reminds me of one of the great learning experiences in my life. I took a trip one Thanksgiving many years ago with Lois to visit her grandfather in Butte, Montana. We were in college at the time and had a new daughter whom her great-grandpa had never met. I remember we came home during a huge snowstorm, one of the worst I can remember. There were hundreds of cars off the road.

On a long, dark stretch of very lonely road I looked down and realized that we were almost out of gas. Have you ever had the experience of watching the gas gauge fall and worrying because there is no service station in sight? As the pressure builds, you realize you are running on fumes. We use fuel to move, and we must have it or we come to a stop.

The power of what Elder Eyring taught is evident in such an experience. We need spiritual energy to progress, and we must have it or we come to a stop. Watching the needle drop when we're not in a position to replenish our spiritual supply is a cause for serious distress. "Great faith has a short shelf life."

On that snowy night I found myself on an unfamiliar stretch of road, responsible for a young wife and a new baby. I really didn't know how far it was to the next gas station. I found myself wishing I had been wiser and paid more attention to my fuel.

Because we don't know when the storm is coming, we

must take every opportunity we have to top off the tank. If we top off our spiritual tanks whenever we can, we will be better prepared for those unfamiliar stretches of dark road and the storms that will surely come.

Knowing Him by Heart

As a young man, I learned a vital lesson about the familiar assurance that preparation brings. One of my friends was practicing the piano for a recital. We wanted him to come out and play ball. His mom told us that he couldn't come out and play until he knew his performance piece "by heart." I didn't really know what that meant, so I asked her what it meant to know something by heart.

She said: "When you know something by heart, it means you are so comfortable with it that no matter what the pressure of performance is, you will do what you have prepared to do perfectly. If somehow you get lost or distracted, you know what is next and can pick right up. If you know a piece by heart, you don't have to constantly watch your hands and worry about what is coming next. When you know something by heart, you have no need to be afraid."

God's plan is that we come to know him by heart. When I know what he would do if he were in my shoes, and then I do it, I'm confident that the outcome of my actions will be positive. The feeling I have about him when I know him by heart is not one of compelled obedience or coercion. It is more the calm understanding that comes from being prepared to succeed.

If you know by heart what he expects of you, when you are called upon to do your part, you will contribute and feel good about it. It doesn't matter *who* you are, but *how* you are. Everyone has a different part. Our peace comes from doing our own individual part as our Father would have us do it.

I remember being taught this for the first time in the reminder from President David O. McKay, "Whate'er thou art, act well thy part." When we know our part by heart, we feel prepared and peaceful. Doing what we know is the right thing to do builds confidence. That confidence allows us to be comfortable with who we are even as the storms of the adversary swirl around us.

The fruits of this preparation for peace are at the core of a favorite quote of mine, which I have framed in my office to remind me of how I wish to live every day: "Quiet minds cannot be perplexed or frightened, but go on in fortune or misfortune at their own private pace, like a clock during a thunderstorm" (Robert Louis Stevenson).

The Savior taught us that the first great commandment is this: "Thou shalt love the Lord thy God with all thy heart, and with all thy soul, and with all thy mind" (Matthew 22:37). It is no accident that *heart* comes first. When we love our Father with all our hearts, we come to know his heart. We know that loving self and neighbor is what he would do. When we know him by heart, we come to understand not only what he would do but why he would do it. His motivation is always love. When we understand why and how we should perform, we can make the music he intended for us to make without having to watch our hands and worry constantly about what is going to happen next.

Remember the seminary answer? Chances are, you've learned it by heart. Now, let us act upon what is in our hearts, believe as little children, replenish our spiritual stores whenever possible, and learn our Father's will for us. Then when the great question assails our lives, "Why this?" we will be in tune to understand and overcome.

Chapter 6

Recognizing Physical Constraints

One of the reasons we might find ourselves asking the great question of "Why this?" is that we deal not only with the impact of our choices and the choices of others, but we deal also with life in a fallen place, mortal and separate from God. Some of our greatest pains come not from sin but just from plain old mortality.

Our physical condition has a profound impact on how we experience life and how we act. We get sick, and in this earthly state that is a fact of life and death. As a people we do a pretty good job of dealing with most illness. We are generally well-intentioned and caring with others. Even though the losses we experience when people die may never heal completely, we find comfort in God's plan of happiness.

However, we do have a tendency to judge ourselves and others more harshly when it comes to depression or other seemingly psychological issues. We don't do very well dealing with these maladies or even recognizing them as physical ailments. A list of these tricky physical challenges could include depression, anxiety, bipolar disorder, schizophrenia, exhaustion, learning disabilities, ADD, ADHD, PMS, and a host of others.

These apparently psychological problems can be caused by or come from the condition and working order of our bodies, including our basic brain and body chemistry. Judging these illnesses as character flaws or as emotional weaknesses is inaccurate and fruitless.

Whether the damage done by unfair judgments is self-inflicted or comes from others, the outcome is just as devastating. A brief list of the all-too-common carnage could include:

"If I had more faith or just worked harder, I would be okay."

"Why doesn't she just snap out of it?"

"If she just had a happy attitude, she would have more energy."

"He just doesn't seem to care."

"She can sound so cheerful on the phone; why can't she be that way all the time?"

"Why doesn't he just apply himself?"

"If he tried harder, school would not be that tough."

"I wasn't lazy before we got married—I am just letting myself go."

Why did President Kimball have so many surgeries when he was an apostle and later as the prophet? Why did our beloved Elder Neal Maxwell have to experience the devastation of chemotherapy? No faith? Not working hard enough? No. It was because they had physical problems that demanded medical interventions. We all live in a mortal condition, and illness is a consequence of that condition.

What we are talking about is just as physical and just as real. For example, biochemical depression is no less physical in its origins and treatments than cancer, a broken bone, or diabetes. What unfeeling person would encourage a child with a broken leg to just get more faith and walk normally? After all, we can't see the break—perhaps it's all in his head.

I am not a physician; I am a counselor. If I have somebody come into my office who has the measles, I don't sit the person down and say, "Let's talk about the red dots." It wouldn't do any good. We could talk forever and I still couldn't talk them out of the measles. Guess what: I can't talk a person out of schizophrenia, either. I can't talk them out of physiological depression. I can't talk them out of PMS or any other physical illness. These are physical issues, not poor behavioral choices or character flaws.

Schizophrenia is a perfect example of a condition that is most often purely physical. Who wants to wake up in the morning and hear strange voices from another place or see people who aren't there or believe the buildings are alive and moving? This isn't something we would choose to do; there is no benefit in that choice. That kind of hallucination, that kind of visual and auditory imagery, is all about brain chemistry that isn't working properly.

Are there some kinds of depression that are purely psychosocial in their origins? Yes. But many more cases have predominantly physiological components. So, in order to better understand what we are dealing with, I might say to a client, "Sit down and tell me why you are depressed."

He then tells me what he sees in his life as problematic: "My mom just died, my girlfriend hates me, and my car broke down. I can't find a job. And I hate the rain."

I say, "Let's go to work and deal with some of that stuff. Let's see if you can't change in some way and relieve some of the hurt and pressure. Let's see if we can alter a situation or two, or view some of this in a healthier way." That seems like a really reasonable thing for a counselor to do.

But more often than not, when I ask what there is in the client's life that is causing this magnitude of depressed feelings, the person will say something like, "Kim, I don't know. I have a good life. I have lots to be thankful for, but when I get up in the morning everything is black and bleak, and I just don't have any energy." Or it might sound like this: "I am just worthless. I am afraid of everything and I am out of options." When I hear responses like those, the very first thing I think is, "Let's call a psychiatrist." Why? Because psychiatrists are medical professionals trained to deal with these kinds of issues specifically. The problem is likely, at least in part, medical. As pharmacologists, psychiatrists can help patients find the connection between how they are feeling and what is going on in their bodies. After that connection is found, a medical intervention can be developed. In the case of depression, for example, an appropriate antidepressant can be identified and administered.

Many times, someone who has been depressed for a long time has issues to deal with as a consequence of that long-term depression, even after he starts feeling better. Habits and coping strategies that have been helpful in dealing with the challenges of the disorder may need to change. Confidence and self-esteem may need to be rebuilt. But none of that can effectively happen until the biochemical source of the malady has been taken care of.

I think we are blessed to live at a time when help is available. There are two things we can do to lessen the impact of these problems in our lives. First, we need to be less judgmental with ourselves and others when it comes to any type of illness. Next, whether it is you or someone you love who is suffering, psychologically expressed physical issues are real medical problems and deserve real medical interventions. Please seek good, capable medical help, particularly in the case of depression.

VIRTUOUS EXHAUSTION

I can't count the number of times I have heard people say something like this: "I don't understand why I am so tired," or, "I used to get so much more done." The truth is that often when those people take the time to add up what they are doing, it is easy to see why they are tired. Despite what they think, frequently they are doing more than ever before.

A young mother I counseled with recently would be a perfect and fairly typical example. She began: "I think I am going crazy. I am tired all the time. I have this great husband and wonderful kids and should be on top of the world. I read my scriptures and say my prayers, I do my Primary job and try to be the best mom and wife I can. What is wrong with me, and what can I do? I had a physical, and the doctor says I am fine. I'm not anemic, and my thyroid is good. I am taking vitamins and eating whole-wheat bread—what else can I do? My husband says I am no fun anymore, and I think he is right."

After this brief exchange, I realize what this woman suffers from is a case of "virtuous exhaustion." I summon up my most counselor-like demeanor and say, "You need more sleep."

She looks at me through bleary eyes and starts to cry. She knows it is true and would love to believe she heard me correctly. However, she won't go down without a fight. She responds: "In college I could stay up as late as I wanted. I lived on pizza and chips and was still always ready at a moment's notice to have some fun."

So I go in for the kill. I ask, "Who cooked the pizza? Did you ever take a Saturday catch-up nap? Did you sleep all night without feeding a baby? Did you ever miss an 8:00 A.M. class and just roll over and have an 'oh my gosh is it really 2:00 P.M.' day? When you went home for Thanksgiving, did you take dirty laundry for Mom to 'help' with? How many kids did you have to take to the doctor or to piano lessons?

"You are tired. Let's find a way to get you some rest."

Whether exhaustion is a product of some medical problem like depression or the natural result of doing too much is irrelevant. What is important to understand is that rest is required for health, and health is required for us to be productive and happy. We often mistakenly see a life of enduring to the end to be about virtuous exhaustion. We get trapped in the subtle web of "the more we do, the better God likes us." That is not true. Life is about making the best of our time and talents here on earth. It is about wisdom and joy as well as production. We all have more worthy and good opportunities available to us than anyone can take advantage of.

For example, if you love to waterski, and there is a perfect day and a perfect lake reserved for you, that would seem to be a recipe for enjoyment. But what if you have just finished running a marathon? Your muscles are spent, your blood sugar is low, and you are dehydrated and hovering near complete exhaustion. Your best friend rings the doorbell and says, with the perkiest of intonations, "Let's hit the lake!"

At this point you would much rather hit your friend. Have you changed? Do you hate waterskiing? Has waterskiing changed? Will it never be fun again? Your physical condition has made the difference. You are just too tired to want to go waterskiing.

We must learn to balance our load better if we can, knowing that this is not always possible. Life can be very demanding, and many of the demands we have are demands we want to meet. We all have good things we need to do that are unbelievably time- and energy-consuming—how about rearing children, pursuing an education, or being a bishop, for example? The challenge is to make the changes in our lives that will make exhaustion the exception, not the rule. The biggest obstacle we face here may be guilt. The antidote for that is understanding that God loves us and has even warned us not to run faster or farther than we have the strength to do (Mosiah 4:27; D&C 10:4).

Women in particular need to find a way to get the rest they need during the most challenging times in their lives. Ask for help (oh, the weakness). Trade nap times with a friend by tending each other's children. Say no to some stuff even if it means being revealed as mortal. Be as kind to yourself as you would be to those you visit teach.

We must be sensitive, as friends, spouses, and leaders, to look for chances to provide ourselves and those we care about with some much-needed rest. We need to concentrate our efforts on those projects and passions that matter most. To paraphrase Elder Neal A. Maxwell, we need to avoid majoring in minor things. By picking our battles, communicating our needs, recognizing our limitations, and acknowledging the limitations of those we love, we can improve our effectiveness.

If we learn to take spiritual and physical nourishment from what we do accomplish rather than exhaust ourselves worrying about what we don't get done, the net result will be a blessing to us and to everyone we love.

It is not easy to learn to trust ourselves as we try to make these hard choices regarding our time and resources. May I suggest a simple test? In the same situation, what counsel would you give your child? That loving parental judgment will always be the right balance. The One who judges us, the One we seek to be more like, is, after all, a perfect and loving parent.

The physical challenges of mortality can be hard! But if we will be wise and seek the Spirit's guidance, we can overcome or learn to endure our physical constraints and get the most out of our lives.

CHAPTER 7

Gratitude: A Tool for Happiness

*B*ecause we have been taught so much about giving and sharing, we become pretty good servers. We learn to be sensitive enough to notice the needs of others and to help. Service is a wonderful gift.

We need a little work on receiving, though. Have you ever given somebody a gift at Christmastime, for example, and could tell from the look in their eyes that they were disappointed? No matter how hard they tried to be excited, you could tell it wasn't what they wanted. Half of the joy in giving a gift is sharing in the emotion of the person receiving the gift.

I remember being particularly mad at my daughters for not being more grateful. Lois and I both grew up in really humble circumstances, and it was my belief that the girls had begun to feel entitled to things. They had cheer-leading and school musicals; they had cars to drive and opportunities to travel. I remember being almost incensed that they weren't more grateful for the many things we had given them. My wife, as always more insightful and tender than I am, made an interesting comment. She said, "Kim, you worked your whole life so they wouldn't know what it was like to be poor, and now you're mad that they don't know what it is like to be poor." She was right, of course, and the girls have grown into sensitive and kind women with appreciative balance in their lives.

This experience and Lois's wise observation introduced me to an interesting pattern. I came to appreciate the need to understand the relationship between awareness and gratitude. Our circumstances make us aware, in various degrees, of the gifts we receive from God. That awareness gives us the opportunity for gratitude. Sometimes it takes some kind of trial or hard life experience to sensitize us to the gifts of God. When these hard things are happening, it can be difficult to see them as gifts or blessings. To make it more difficult, it can take a long time to understand whether a particular experience is a blessing or not.

For example, I remember going into the mission field thinking I was very poor. My family didn't have a lot of money—and we lived in a part of town where there was a lot of wealth. That comparison left me feeling poor and picked on. My life experience on my mission changed my thinking very quickly. I had been in the mission field less than one day when I walked into a hogan on the Navajo reservation that changed my understanding. Based on that sweet experience, I redefined the difference between want and need. After coming to know these good people, I also came to appreciate that money or worldly possessions were not required for happiness or success. My mission experience taught me to look for what God valued. I began to appreciate character and to prize the attributes and experiences that develop it.

I realized that what I had thought of as a blessing might not always be a blessing. What I experienced as a trial was not always a trial, either. The line between blessing and curse got a little harder to define. I know many have had that same experience.

As we become more aware of the subtle differences between blessings and challenges and gifts, the question we ask ourselves often changes from "Why me?" to "What can I learn?" or "Is it possible there is a blessing here?" What I know by my experience is the condition of the Father's heart. God's heart is always inclined toward loving us, and that keeps me looking for the blessing. I am reminded of Nephi's response to the question asked him by the Spirit: "And he said unto me: Knowest thou the condescension of God? And I said unto him: I know that he loveth his children; nevertheless, I do not know the meaning of all things" (1 Nephi 11:16–17).

By starting with the right assumption, we get the right vision. Because God loves me, he allows me to bless my life and the lives of others with my choices. If I start with that assumption, my capacity for awareness and gratitude increases dramatically.

I often reflect on the example of my wife. She is always looking for the lesson and seems to be grateful for even the smallest opportunity to see it. I can picture her at some task when one of our daughters would walk in with a dandelion behind her back. Lois would take the weed as if it were gold. I can't tell you the number of times we've had dinner with a dandelion bouquet as a centerpiece. Lois saw the heart, not the weed. When we receive a gift, we need to see the heart as well as what is in the package.

We need to look for why an experience or opportunity is given. That will also help us when we give. Sometimes our children don't have the experience to know that what we are sharing with them is a gift. I can't believe, for example, that when we offer them an opportunity to do yard work, the word *gift* or *blessing* doesn't automatically jump into the minds of our children.

Perhaps it is the same reason that when we have a ward welfare assignment, or get to lose money on a business venture, the character tests we experience don't feel like gifts or blessings at first. However, if we start with the right assumption, we often get the better vision.

Plain and Precious Things

The scriptures talk about the plain and precious things and how important they are. Yet when was the last time any of us really wanted to be plain and precious? I think it is important to remember that Heavenly Father delights in simple beauty and in honesty and integrity. When we delight in those things, we come to know Heavenly Father better.

It's interesting to notice how often the things we hear about people at their funerals are those plain and precious things. The stories and insights we get at funerals are the parables of those being remembered. If we paid attention to those daily things in our lives, we would discover it is the plain and simple things that give us character. We become who we are by responding to our choices and challenges, our options and obligations.

We need to pay attention to our lives and the lives of others *before* our funerals. We must learn to observe and to be taught. If this life is the time to learn, we need to start asking ourselves as we go, "What can I learn from this?" or "How can I use this experience to grow?" Life will give us the answers if we will be introspective and open to the Spirit. We need to be aware of what we really like, what and who we care about, and what interests us. We miss so much when we don't pay attention to the sweet and common blessings and challenges we experience daily.

EXPECTATION IS THE MOTHER OF SATISFACTION

Why is it important to recognize our blessings and opportunities? Why is it important to have a realistic view of this earthly test and of our limitations? Why is it valuable to see a loving and benevolent Father as well as the challenges of our condition? These views help us establish our expectations of how our life can be.

I remember preparing a talk and thinking I could call it "Expectation Is the Mother of Satisfaction." As I thought it through, I realized that I could also call my talk "Expectation Is the Mother of Disappointment." What we expect, not what happens, is often the key to whether we are satisfied or disappointed.

For example, imagine somebody comes up to you and hands you a thousand dollars with this explanation: "You won a prize—here's a thousand dollars." You'd be elated! It would be a wonderful gift. Now let's say instead that somebody says, "You've won one of two prizes, ten million dollars or a thousand dollars. Choose door number one or door number two." You choose and get the thousand-dollar door. How would you feel?

It is the same thousand dollars!

Seeing something as a blessing instead of a stroke of luck or an entitlement, for example, changes how we feel about what we receive. When we see obedience as an opportunity, we experience it differently than when we see it as slavery. Is service a project or a blessing? Is parenthood a necessary obligation or a chance to have a fulness of joy?

Our faith and understanding are important components for interpreting what we experience and observe. What we have been taught about life by our experiences, and how we choose to respond to those experiences, are fundamental to our sense of disappointment or satisfaction.

I asked an incest survivor to make a list of questions she would like to ask God about men. She expected all men to be unkind and violent. At the same time, she believed her Father in Heaven was a good and loving being. This was very confusing. She wanted to know why all men were so flawed. She wanted to know how God had made them, what characteristics he had given them. She wanted to know how men felt about women and if any of them could be trusted. One of the compound questions she wrote to God is particularly telling. (I use it here with permission.)

"Do men really love women or do they just want them? Do they need them, or are we just a necessary responsibility?"

After all she had been through, and with her self-esteem in shreds, she still had faith enough to ask her Father in Heaven to help her set her expectations based on heavenly parameters. She asked to know, even though her experience with the world would have kept her isolated and bitter. She chose to look for a reason to keep trying, and she found it.

Agency is the gift of a loving Father. Even when the influence of the adversary has caused others to choose poorly and hurt us, we have the right and power to respond how we will. If we know the road will be rough, we can prepare with that in mind.

Choosing Our Own Reactions

The descriptive labels that loving people give us—or those we give ourselves—should be positive and constructive. They should reflect our identity as children of God. There are other voices that try to define us in ways that are not so uplifting. These negative labels are the constructs of the adversary, designed to confuse or mislead us. If we accept them, they undermine our confidence and disguise our true identity.

One of the most effective examples of affirmative labels I know is the Young Women's theme. It is self-definition at its very best. It is both the declaration of a loving and supportive community and an affirmation of self. It is no accident that the prophet endorses that theme, which begins, "We are daughters of our Heavenly Father, who loves us, and we love Him." There is the promise of safety and peace in that calm assurance of who we are. It is up to us to be comfortably firm in our testimony of who and what we are.

One of my favorite illustrations of this principle is

found in an oft-told story from Zen folklore. It is the story of the wise swordsman.

There was once a great swordsman who had with time become a teacher of the truth as well as the sword. He was very old but was still a master of the blade.

One day a young challenger looking for a reputation as a swordsman arrived in the village and challenged the old master to fight. The young man knew that if he could be the first to defeat the teacher he would be famous. It was with this hope that he challenged the old man.

The young challenger was not without skill. He had the keen ability to spot and exploit any weakness in an opponent. The opponent's first move would always reveal such a weakness. The young challenger would then strike with amazing force and lightning speed. He had won every match he had been in by using this skill of exploiting the very first move of his opponent.

The master understood the challenger's reputation. He was aware of the strength of the young man. To the surprise of many, the teacher agreed to the challenge.

As the two prepared for battle, the old warrior assumed a comfortable attitude, with his sword in the ready position, and waited. In an effort to provoke the master to make that first move, the young warrior began to insult the old man. He belittled him in every conceivable way. He abused him with every curse and insult one could imagine. The old warrior just stood still, comfortable with his sword in the ready position and a very slight smile on his face. After a long time the young warrior was exhausted. He knew he was beaten and slunk slowly from the courtyard in shame.

The curious students gathered around their master, asking, "How could you allow such insults?" The swordsman and teacher considered the questions carefully and responded with a question of his own:

"If someone offers you a gift and you do not receive it, to whom does the gift still belong?"

We have no obligation to believe the insults and denigrating comments of the world and the adversary. We can find the strength to withstand those lies by knowing the truth about who and what we are. We can become confident and stand comfortably in almost any circumstance when we know our loving Father stands beside us.

Viktor Frankl, who spent time incarcerated in a concentration camp during World War II, shared his experience with that kind of strength: "We who lived in concentration camps can remember the men who walked through the huts comforting others, giving away their last piece of bread. They may have been few in number, but they offer sufficient proof that everything can be taken from a man but one thing: the last of the human freedoms—to choose one's attitude in any given set of circumstances" (*Man's Search for Meaning* [New York: Simon and Schuster, 1963], 104).

The choice is up to us. If we decide that every day is just one more hard thing to do, that's exactly how we'll face the day. If we can see every day as a gift from God, we get up feeling like it's our birthday.

But if we have been mired in habits of negative thinking, how can we change?

THE POWER OF GRATITUDE

Developing a sense of gratitude has long been a tool used by counselors and business, spiritual, and community leaders to motivate people and to effectively advocate and sustain change. We are strengthened in our resolve by feelings of gratitude. Gratitude empowers us by helping us understand the resources we can bring to bear in overcoming the challenges of life.

May I suggest three proven activities to use as gratitude-enhancing tools to help us get more peace and happiness from our lives? I am not implying that you have to incorporate all three into your life as a comprehensive plan for happiness and peace. That would be great, but even doing one will help. Look at your circumstances and decide if you can use any or all of these tools. I promise each is beneficial.

First, I suggest making a habit of grateful prayer. In one of your prayers each day, don't ask for anything. Make it a prayer of thanks.

Many years ago, a wise stake president by the name of

Gordon Conger asked us as a high council to go a week without asking for anything in our prayers. He suggested we take one week and thank Heavenly Father daily for all we had.

I noticed several things as I was obedient to his counsel. I noticed that my prayers got a whole lot longer. My awareness of my blessings grew as I began to list what I was thankful for, and it got to be great fun. I really enjoyed those prayers. It was almost embarrassing to recognize how much I had to be grateful for that I may have failed to acknowledge in the past.

I found myself feeling a lot closer to Heavenly Father because I truly realized how kind he was to me. I began to see him as a loving and benevolent Father. As the week went on, I became more aware of how much my family and other loved ones meant to me. I became more and more in touch with all the blessings I experienced through my association with them. I noticed that my prayers became more about people and less about stuff.

I must confess here, though, that as I contemplated what to thank God for, I learned how much I appreciated a good meal, a good book, and a good nap.

That is the first tool. Every day, for whatever period of time you decide on, say one prayer that is nothing but thanks.

The second tool I recommend to increase our awareness of what we have to be grateful for is an extension of those prayers. Whether you start a computer document, or set aside a special place in your journal, or have a little notebook tucked away somewhere, I suggest you begin recording what you have recognized as blessings in your life.

I think the blessings we see in the lives of those we love should also be included. It is important to write our observations down because we tend to forget specifics in the forward rush of our lives. As time passes, we forget, for example, how thankful we were for Heavenly Father's help with a specific test at school. (Heck, I forget I ever *took* the test.) We forget how thankful we were that our child's injury didn't turn out to be more serious. We forget the joy we felt in our silent prayer of recognition when we heard that our husband did get that new job. As time goes by, we forget the myriad blessings we have received. We lose track of prayers answered.

It is the nature of this earthly trial that it keeps coming at us. As a result, we focus on the current challenge we face or the pain a loved one feels today. There is always a new leak to be fixed or a demand we had not anticipated. When we keep a list of the blessings we have experienced, our current challenges fall into perspective. Reading that list also gives us hope, and that is a medicine we can all use a little more of.

The final tool for developing gratitude is a written one as well. How you note it doesn't matter. Some people

prefer computers; others love to write longhand. No matter how you do it, what I suggest is finding a way to keep
track of the lessons you have learned from the people in
your life.

My greatest lessons have come in the parables of every-
day life. It has been my experience that when we look
back on our lives, we remember the impact of certain
people. These are the people who did something that we
valued or who touched us in some special way. Whether
it was with a skill, a talent, a teaching, or a characteristic,
they changed us.

It doesn't take much of a note to keep track of what we
learned from these mentors in our lives. Often a sentence
or two will be enough to help us remember these special
people and the gifts they gave. As we read through these
recollections, we'll be reminded of what has been important in our lives.

I have kept such a list of what I have gained from
others for many years, and it has been a valuable tool. The
thing that jumps out as I review it is how many of the
things that had the greatest impact on me were little
things. Let me give you a couple of examples:

The first is a one-line quote from a man who was in
the stake presidency when I was called to be a bishop. As a
new bishop, I asked him for advice with a struggle I was
having to help a couple overcome some serious problems.
Here is the advice he gave me: "Get them to pray, Bishop.

Prayer and sin don't live in the same house." I have used that principle a hundred times to help people open the shutters and feel the light of Christ. Prayer and sin don't live in the same house.

I have several observations in my notes about what my grandma did to touch me and teach me. I hope I am like her when it comes to loving as the Savior loves. She was a great example of the staying power of love. I was eight when she died, but I still remember how important she made me feel. Here is some of what I have noted about her:

It didn't matter who else was in the room, it didn't matter what time of the day or night it was, or if she was sick or well, when I walked in the room, she always acknowledged me. That interest made me feel valuable.

She talked to me as if I understood what she was saying. She always dealt with me like I was a friend. She was willing to explain anything I asked her as best she could.

She always asked me to help pick raspberries and lilacs and made me feel useful. She taught me to treat everyone as if they were important. I have found that to be a real gift. It is a guiding principle in my experience.

Here is another life lesson my record has helped me keep alive: My Grandpa Nelson ended every meal with these words: "Thanks for mine." It didn't matter what it was or who cooked it or who we were with, at the end of the meal he would say, "Thanks for mine." He had known real hunger and poverty in his life. That experience taught him to be thankful. He was always grateful in whatever he did. He was grateful for his food; he was grateful for his job; he was grateful for a good day of fishing.

I find that I am willing to do almost anything for someone who is grateful. It not only makes me feel good but it helps me understand that the person is getting some value, some benefit, or some blessing from my action.

This simple note from my file leads me to remember one last example:

Bishop Melvin Peterson
Orem 37th Ward
"President, teach them they only have to decide to go to priesthood once."

Here is what that note helps me recall: Melvin Peterson was a great bishop. He was one of the men in my life who taught me the most about the gospel. He was the kind of man I wanted to be when I grew up, somebody who lifted all those around him.

He called me to be the Young Men's president and priests quorum advisor. That would be a job I was destined to have a lot throughout my life, but this was my first experience with it. I believe I was twenty-two or twenty-three years old, not much older than the young men with whom I worked. I prayerfully considered what I could do to be a better advisor. I decided I had better be sure I knew what it was that Bishop Peterson would like me to be teaching the young men.

One day in quorum presidency meeting I asked him, "Bishop, what one lesson would you like me to teach these young men?"

He kind of chuckled and said, "Now, this is going to sound a little simple, but more than anything else, I want the boys to understand how many times in their lives they have to decide to go to priesthood meeting."

I must have looked a little blank. It was clear to him I didn't understand what he was saying. He chuckled again in his loving way and taught me. "Brother Nelson, we only have to decide to do the right thing in our lives one time. I'm not strong enough to decide every Sunday morning that priesthood is important, especially if I've had a rough night or a rough week and am exhausted. I don't know if after that challenge I can trust myself to decide the next morning with a clear head whether or not priesthood is important to me.

"So I decided to pray about it and determine once and for all whether or not to attend priesthood. I prayed about it and I decided that I would. And for the rest of my life, that's a decision I don't have to burden myself with. I've already made it and there's no need to make it again."

Over the years, the lesson I taught my priests and retaught my priests was this: Whenever we decide to do the right thing—attend church, build our testimonies, read our scriptures, or whatever it is—we have to decide only once. With that decision made, the rest of the time all we have to do is what we have already decided to do. That lesson from Bishop Peterson has made my life a lot easier.

Here, in review, are the three tools we've discussed to develop gratitude and the peace and happiness that flow from it:

1. Say one prayer a day that is a prayer of thanks only. Don't ask for anything.

2. Keep a cumulative record of the gifts and blessings you have recognized from your loving Father in Heaven. This list will remind you of the magnitude of that love and put the current demands of life in a more realistic perspective.

3. Finally, keep track of what you have learned from the people in your life. It will remind you of great lessons and great people who may otherwise be lost.

Gratitude is a wonderful key to having the happiest life possible!

CHAPTER 8

The Benefit of the Doubt

*O*ne of the facts of our earthly life is that even those of us with the best of intentions are not perfect. Remember, no one learns to ride a bike without suffering a few falls. As we're striving to get the most out of life despite our shortcomings, one question we might ask ourselves is: How do we handle failure? What do we do when someone we love falls short? What if that "someone" is us?

One response to a loved one's imperfect performance is to take the attitude, "No one can be trusted." If trust is an ongoing issue for us, for whatever reason, we need to be sure we don't take an all-or-nothing stance about it. It's tempting to run to our absolute "no one can be trusted" setting at the slightest hint of failure by someone we have begun to trust. We need to remember that insensitivity or poor judgment does not always mean that a person really doesn't care about us.

Let me give you an example. Two of my favorite women are my wife, Lois, and her sweet friend Jane. Jane's husband and I were bishops at the same time. We apparently had another experience in common: We were bishops who were less than perfect in recognizing our need to spend some quality time with our wives.

Both Lois and Jane handled the challenge of our insensitive behavior effectively, with some humor and understanding. It would have been easy for them to assume that they were unimportant to us. The default could have been, "Here we go again. My needs are just not important enough for him to care. If he really loved me, he would know how much I need him."

The reality for me was that, in an effort to be the best bishop I could be, I had slipped into the habit of putting some of the wrong things first. Jane's husband, Don, had done the same thing. As we reflected on it years later, we both realized that we needed the time with our wives at least as much as they needed us—probably more.

Bless their hearts for giving us the benefit of the doubt in terms of our commitment to them. They believed we loved them in spite of our less-than-perfect performance. Here is how they handled our failure.

Jane placed a call to the bishop's office during bishopric meeting one night and asked to speak to the bishop. She was polite, sweet, and gentle. Lovingly she said, "Bishop, this is Sister Pugh." (Remember, she was speaking to her husband.) She went on: "My husband will not come home to me. What do you suggest I do?" The bishop wisely concluded the meeting and went to check on Sister Pugh and her foolish husband.

When I was the bishop and making less-than-perfect choices about my time with my wife, Lois handled it this way. She called my executive secretary and made an appointment. She asked if he would just note her scheduled time as "new sister in the ward." In she walked and said cheerfully, "I thought perhaps if I made an appointment we might get to talk." How loving and kind she was as she called me to repentance and gave me a chance to improve.

Everybody makes mistakes. I am so grateful Lois didn't assume that I couldn't improve or didn't want to. We need to provide those we love with the help they need to do better. I can't demonstrate my willingness to try harder if I am not aware of how I have been hurtful or insensitive. Giving someone the benefit of the doubt, and then lovingly correcting or reminding them, can build trust and help them overcome weaknesses.

THE BISHOP AND THE FUNERAL

How we choose to respond to the unwitting mistakes of others affects both us and them. We can always choose the loving or positive response. One of my favorite stories about the effect of a charitable choice has to do with a young bishop in Salt Lake City who was dealing with the pressures of a new calling, young children, and a demanding career. In a time well before cell phones, he experienced a potentially devastating communications problem regarding a funeral at which he was to preside.

The bishop had been up late for several nights helping the family plan the program and coordinate the arrangements for the funeral, which was scheduled for Saturday morning. Somehow he became confused about the starting time for the service and arrived an hour and a half late. He drove into the church parking lot just as the casket was being taken to the hearse.

He was to have presided and to have shared some comments at this funeral for a woman he felt great love and kindness toward. He was brokenhearted when he realized the mistake he had made. His first thought was, "If only the old bishop, whom everybody loved, had still been the one in charge. A real bishop never would have made such an obvious and hurtful error."

He got out of the car and started quickly toward the church. The first person he made eye contact with was the husband of the woman who was being buried. That good friend and brother threw his arms around him and said, "Oh, bishop, we're so glad you're safe. We were worried something had happened to you. Would you please join us and preside at the graveside?"

The young bishop told me this story thirty years after

his dear friend's funeral. Those thirty years of dedicated service were made more effective by the choice of a husband in his hour of grief. That husband chose to be kind to a priesthood leader who had made a mistake.

My friend shared with me how that kindness had changed his feelings about himself and about forgiveness. He had come to know in that moment that, no matter what the circumstance, there is always room for kindness. He was taught to assume the best until proven otherwise. The value of one kind word when an honest mistake had been made was obvious. It allowed him to feel much better about himself, and it also made it easier for him to accept the honest mistakes of others.

"She Thinks You Are So Great!"

We need to feel appreciated and valued, whether we think we deserve it or not. I once counseled a couple who unfortunately chose to be divorced. About two years later, they called and asked if I would help them review and revise their parenting plan. They had worked on it and it was obvious to both of them that things needed to be modified a little. I was flattered that they both trusted me to be honest and caring enough to help in the process.

I observed an interesting life lesson when we met for the first time. The husband had remarried recently in the temple. His new wife was not someone he had known at the time of the divorce. His ex-wife was obviously still bitter and angry. It is my experience that this kind of bitterness is not a gender issue, nor is it necessarily related specifically to how much time has gone by. It is about feeling like a victim.

As they sat on the couch and we worked through the parenting plan, her frustration just grew and grew. Finally she almost exploded with this question: "*How* can you be so happy and okay?" She continued in a fit of absolute bile, "It's *her,* isn't it? The only reason you married that woman is because she thinks you are so great."

There was an uncomfortable pause. Then he turned to her and said, "Duh!"

We all need to have regular contact with people who think we are so great. If more husbands and wives would demonstrate those kinds of feelings for each other, there would be fewer divorces in the world! Looking for the good instead of the bad in people is a formula for happiness.

How Are You Treating Yourself? A Test

It is easy to respond positively to those who serve and love us. It is less easy to respond well to people whose mistakes make them seem uncaring. But hardest of all may be to treat ourselves well in spite of our own imperfect performance. I'd like to propose a little test—just one question—that will help you see how worthy you are to receive somebody's love, recognition, encouragement, or kindness, despite your weaknesses. It is also a way to measure how severe your own self-judgment should be. It is the master question from which most people have a tough time escaping.

Here is the question: "If you saw a mother treating her daughter the way you treat yourself, what kind of mother would you think she is?"

Let me give you some examples of the disparity between what you know to be healthy for those you love and how you treat yourself.

Picture yourself with your daughter, sitting on her bed. She has been crying. You have asked her several times what the problem is. She decides with some difficulty to share her broken heart, even though at your age you could surely never understand. She starts telling you about Rick. He was at the dance tonight and didn't even look at her. Not only that, but he kept staring at Tina Balinski as if she were some kind of princess.

Is this a big deal? It is to her, and you know it. She is important to you, and that makes it important no matter what the subject is. What would your advice to her sound like? Would it be, "Get over it"? Would you say, "Grow up," or "I thought it was something serious"? If you responded in that way, how many more bedside chats could you expect to have with this daughter?

What if your daughter gave a less-than-stellar talk in sacrament meeting? What if her Primary lesson didn't go well? How would you handle that? My guess is you would be encouraging and recognize her efforts and the other demands on her time. You would reassure her of your love and of Father in Heaven's affection for her as well.

What would happen if in spite of your warnings your daughter decided to get a haircut the day of prom and returned home in tears wearing a ball cap? Even in the face of this obvious chance for an "I told you so" moment, what would you do?

What if your daughter came to you worried about some transgression she was going to see the bishop about? If she shared this fear and the reason for it, how would you respond? Would your kind, motherly advice be something like this? "Well, too darn bad, girl. I warned you, but you wouldn't listen. You know everything, don't you, Miss Smarty Pants. You have just ruined eternity for yourself and are headed for destruction. I will think of you from this point on as a big, fat loser. So will your Father in Heaven and the Savior, I'm sure."

You and I both know that your response would sound *nothing* like that. But I know just as surely that some of your inner self-tirades sound that insensitive and worse. In the examples above, what if it had been your talk, or your lesson, rather than your daughter's? Would your self-talk have been as encouraging as the reassurance you would give your daughter? What if it was you who had made a bad choice and had to wear some metaphorical hat to keep your mistake from showing to the world? How many times have you minimized a hurt rather than sharing it with someone who might help? Most people who would show natural tenderness for a daughter's drama or bad hair are merciless with their own imperfections.

I am not suggesting we become too easy on ourselves. We need to keep striving to be better. What I am recommending is the use of this test to help us learn to build and encourage rather than hurt and degrade ourselves. With practice asking the master question, we might even allow some kindness from a friend or some love from heaven to sneak over the "you don't deserve it" wall around our hearts.

This is the magic of the master question: When you remove *you* from the picture, and replace yourself with someone you believe deserves the right response, your advice to that person is generally perfect. It is godly; it is parental. It expresses love and encouragement, without fostering self-judgment or self-loathing.

We all struggle with feelings of unworthiness. In our efforts to make it to the kingdom, we often run into an obstacle that seems disqualifying to us. We feel we have some fatal flaw or weakness that makes it impossible for us to return to our Father. This kind of discouragement is just what the enemy would have us feel. He would whisper, or even shout, if necessary, "You can't succeed; why try?" This is one of the most devastating and successful weapons in the armory of evil.

The real problem with this kind of "I'm already disqualified" thinking is that we lose perspective. We get an imperfection or two stuck in our minds and can't think of anything else. It's like getting a piece of popcorn stuck in your teeth at the movies. Has that ever happened to you? It may be a little thing, but it feels big. The more you think about it, the bigger it seems. Soon you forget the movie; all you can think about is this huge hunk of popcorn stuck in your teeth.

Here is a way to put the potentially damaging foolishness of this kind of thinking into perspective. Suppose you were going into the final judgment—and we all are. How would you like it if your whole life were to be judged by a single event, and Satan got to pick which event it would be? That would not be a good thing, would it? In fact, that would be a bad thing, and yet we do it to ourselves all the time.

Here's what that single-minded self-judgment might sound like for me. Let's say I've got fifteen or twenty-seven really good things going for me in my life, but I'm fat. And, if you will excuse the pun, it feels huge to me.

I get up in the morning, and my day begins with an internal conversation like this. I say to myself, "It's a beautiful (I'm fat) day. I'm going to go to my (I'm fat) job and have some (I'm fat) fun with my (I'm fat) pals. In fact, I can't feel bad about myself because I belong to this really great ward of skinny people, except me (and I'm fat). I have a lovely (I'm fat) wife and wonderful (I'm fat) daughters." As these thoughts permeate my every waking moment, and some of my dreams, I wonder why I can't get over the pervasive feeling that I'm fat. I wonder if that "I'm fat" feeling might have a little bit more power over me than it ought to. So I decide I just need to be a little more positive—well, I'm positive I'm fat!

What I'm doing here is judging myself by *one* parameter, and I didn't pick a good one. In my experience, we don't do a very good job of balancing the positive and negative parts of our lives as we evaluate ourselves. Over and over and over again we pick things to focus on that aren't going to lift us up. Then we wonder why we feel so lousy about ourselves.

This is where we need to begin to measure what God measures. You might think, I don't know what God measures. But you do. You measure what God measures in others all the time. You just don't think to measure those things in yourself.

I can't tell you how many times in counseling I've looked at clients who seemed to see only the negative in themselves and said, "Are you kind?" I ask the question knowing full well the honest answer.

They reply, "Yes, I try to be."

I then ask, "Do you think that matters to God?"

They acknowledge that it does matter—usually with a downward glance, almost as if admitting that doing something that makes Father pleased shows a lack of humility.

I then ask a series of questions to help them become more aware of what God values. These questions and our responses should help each of us come to a very important understanding. We know what God is measuring.

Here are some of those questions:

Are you gentle?
Are you interested in others?
Are you good-hearted?
Are you honest?
Are you willing?
Do you want to do the right thing?
Do you try to be fair?

Every one of these things matters in God's economy. These are the kinds of factors our Father uses to measure our progress and success. Aren't they the things we use all the time to measure the performance or accomplishments of those we care about? The last time I checked, His is the economy that matters most in the end. Unfortunately, the world's economy sometimes shouts a lot louder than God's, and we forget.

One reason it's sometimes difficult to see the positive instead of the negative is that the world we live in can be a scary place, and we have to be aware of that to protect ourselves and those we are responsible for. We are always looking out for trouble, solving problems, and putting out fires. We come into a world where we are taught to avoid mistakes and the pain they bring. From the time we're young, we hear the warnings: "Look both ways," "Don't touch that, it's hot," "Where is your little brother?" and the ever-popular "You could put an eye out!"

Is it any wonder that we have to remind ourselves to be positive? For every silver lining, we have been warned about a hundred dark clouds. Our short-term memory is about survival. We are so intent upon our daily tasks and worries that we need to be reminded that we are not here just to survive but to flourish. We need to concentrate on the search for joy, because our history in this fallen and dangerous place has taught us all about being aware of potential danger and pain.

There is a simple way to test that theory. Just consider: What do we need to be reminded of? Do any of us feel compelled to have a magnet on our fridge that says . . .

"Remember, no matter how bright the day, you still have monster thighs."

"Take time to consider what part of your Church calling is still undone."

"Have you paused today to worry about who your daughter is dating?"

"Remember, sister, no matter how hard you try, the mother always gets the blame."

We need to override the "worry settings" of life by reminding ourselves that this life is not all we have to look forward to and that not everything in this life is fearful or worrisome.

I'm not suggesting putting on rose-colored glasses to see the whole world as sweetness and light. I am suggesting, however, that we take off the garbage-colored ones and try some clear lenses. Well, if I am being perfectly honest, I guess I *would* recommend a little optimistic heavenly tint to counter the negative influences of the environment. Something like polarized lenses to take away the glare of criticism or the harsh light of self-judgment would be a nice touch as well.

We all make mistakes, and our own shortcomings are easy for us to see. It is much easier for me to see what's lovable or valuable about you than it is to see those things about myself.

The first person in my life I really knew loved me was my Grandma Kinghorn. Quite a while ago, I wrote this poem about how she made me feel. Try to feel the impact of one woman's love on the life of one man who was then a little boy. My grandma died when I was eight or so, and yet if I was asked to name the person who had the most influence on my spiritual life, other than my wife or children, it would be my grandma.

A Lesson from Grandma

When I was young, quite small in fact,
I learned a lot it seems

I learned of songs and cookie dough
Of stories and of dreams

And of all the lessons I was taught
The one I best recall

Is one my grandma taught me . . .
Being young don't make you small

She treated me like I was
Up to any test

She taught me what mattered most
Was giving it my best

So when my life is stormy
And my road's a little rough

I remember what my grandma taught me
Being me's enough . . .

When I watch my wife be grandma
And I think of mine, long past

I clearly see the miracle of what
Makes grandma's lessons last

The miracle is simple
When I take the time to see

My grandma loved me every day
Just for being me.

We can identify the loving influence of our mothers and grandmothers, our children and fathers and uncles and aunts and others. But somehow, for some reason, we seem over and over to miss the power there is in loving ourselves.

We can easily see the gentle love and influence of others. We can see the constant concern of parents for their children. We feel the same concern for our kids, sometimes in spite of their behavior, not because of it.

Why, then, surrounded by all this proof, do we judge ourselves so harshly and feel certain our perfect Father in Heaven sees only our weaknesses and faults? Let's not disqualify ourselves from the constant care of a loving Father by focusing on what is negative to the exclusion of all else. We need to have a better perspective than that.

Perspective Can Change the View

When we are evaluating ourselves or our situation, we often don't take the time to get a clear picture. We don't take a broad enough sample of our lives before we make our assessments. It is often the poorest part of our performance that we give all the attention to. It's like looking at a report card that has five A's and a B; we have a hard time giving all six marks equal attention.

Let me give you an example. If I feel overwhelmed, I

might focus solely on what feels so big or difficult. It would be like taking an 8x10 picture of a beautiful scene and evaluating the whole picture by a tiny fragment. Let's just say in the upper right-hand corner of our picture there's a fluffy, grayish-white cumulus cloud. My favorite kind of sky is a beautiful blue one with three or four of those big, puffy clouds floating by. A cloudless sky can be beautiful, but it is not as interesting to me as one with some clouds. If I were to pick a perfect day, that's what the sky would be like. I would be up in the high country, and there would be a beautiful trout stream, of course. The temperature would be about 85 degrees. The fish would be biting and the bugs wouldn't.

In this example, we have taken a picture that represents the beautiful, broad vista of what might be a near-perfect day in our lives. But if we looked only at the small part of the sky in the upper right-hand corner, all we would see would be that grayish cloud. If we assumed that we were seeing the whole sky, it would seem like it is gray, all gray. If that was our whole vision, and we stopped looking, we would miss a beautiful scene and a mostly blue sky. Our world would be gray if that one bit was all we looked at.

That's why the Lord chooses to counsel us about perspective. That's why he invites us to look not only at our earthly time but at the preearthly existence, the judgment, and the possibilities of everything to come. He does this to remind us to draw back and increase the magnitude of what we are able to see or sense. All of a sudden it's not just a gray mist over everything. Our life is not just a cloud. The day is a beautiful, wonderful, magnificent day that we might have missed if we had been focusing only on one little gray part of the much bigger picture.

Our objective, and often our struggle, is to not let those negative parts of our lives keep us from seeing the whole picture. Sure, some of the sky is gray, but some of it is also blue. And there just might be a trout stream only a few feet away if we take the time to look at the whole picture.

Challenge or Blessing?

One reason our perspective is limited is that we don't always recognize a blessing when we see one. Many times, in an effort to understand our earthly condition, we assume that something we did or didn't do is the reason for our blessings or challenges. I can't tell you how many times I have heard people say, "What did I do to deserve this?" This viewpoint almost assumes that the universe and everything in it is controlled by our actions. The dilemmas and "beat myself up" opportunities inherent in that kind of thinking are almost endless.

In reality, it is sometimes even difficult to know what a blessing is and what a curse is. One of my favorite stories to illustrate this point begins with a woman who walked into my office one day while I was serving as a bishop. She was almost ninety. Her husband had died a couple of years before our visit. She and her husband had been extremely close and loved each other very much. She sat down and began to cry. I thought, "Well, she's so lonely, I need to give her a minute to regroup." So I sat quietly and waited. She looked up about a minute later and said, "Bishop, I am so mad I don't know what to do."

"Tell me why," I said, trying to conceal my surprise.

She responded, "I can't figure out what's wrong with me that God doesn't want me."

I thought for a minute and said, "What makes you think that God doesn't want you?"

"Well, he let my husband die more than two years ago. He must have been needed for some important work beyond the veil. Me, on the other hand—apparently there is still some imperfection that I have to get rid of before the Lord needs me. Maybe there's some lesson I've still got to learn, because he just doesn't want me. I pray every night that he will take me, and he just won't do it. I've tried and tried to figure out where I've goofed up, but I just don't know what I've done wrong. What makes me so unworthy or not ready that he would punish me by leaving me here?"

Two or three weeks before this exchange I had met with another woman in my office, about the same age as the sister I just described. Her husband had been dead for several years. She had just found out she was terminally ill and wondered what big sin she had committed that had caused God to come and take her. "Why cut my life short when there is so much help I could provide to those I love here?" she wanted to know. "I feel like Father is disappointed in me somehow."

It has always been interesting to me that when something bad happens—or at least something we perceive to be bad—we find a way to blame God and ourselves in one easy, labor-saving step. Could it be as simple as "I got sick" or "I'm still healthy"? Perhaps there is some larger plan or influence at work that we are unaware of or couldn't possibly be aware of. Who knows! When we presume to have it all figured out, we have created the perfect setting for the adversary to play the blame game. He jumps right in and blames us for some sin or flaw—or he blames God for wanting us to suffer. That kind of thinking gets us to, "God doesn't think I'm very valuable because he put me here in this place where I have all these challenges."

We need to give God the benefit of the doubt and trust that his plan is perfect even if we're not. We need to give others the benefit of the doubt and assume that their mistakes are not aimed personally at making us miserable. And, most of all, we need to give ourselves the benefit of the doubt and be kinder in the way we think of our own progress. As we come to do these things, the way to happiness opens before us.

CHAPTER 9

Making Good Choices

*H*eavenly Father has confidence in our capacity to choose well. He has given us all kinds of guidance to help us along the way. One of the things we need to learn to do is consult our feelings. Most of the time, if we are honestly assessing our deepest feelings, we will know what we should be doing.

Trust, safety, and charity are important feelings for us to get to know. Sometimes the best way to recognize these or any other feelings is to put a name on them. For example, if we feel the Spirit, it's important to say, "This is the Spirit." That way, the next time we feel it, we can identify it more readily. The same is true of feelings like guilt or shame or fear or pride or foolishness. When we identify these negative emotions, we can avoid the things that create them and are not healthy for us. Knowing what generates our feelings, good or bad, increases our ability to choose those things or people that are beneficial for us and to avoid those that are not.

My favorite illustration of this is a children's game I'll bet you've played in a Primary or school class. It's the "Hot and Cold" game. One person is sent from the room, and the rest of the children hide an object. Everybody knows its location except the person looking for it. The children who know where the object is hidden then become a source of information for the searcher. The closer the hunter gets to the hidden object, the louder everyone says, "Hotter, hotter, hotter," and the farther away, "Colder, colder, colder."

When we recognize and trust our feelings, what we experience can be an extension of that very same game. If we are willing to be honest with ourselves and move toward the good we feel and actively avoid those choices that lead us away from the light, we will find the hidden peace we seek. We know the way. We must come to trust our feelings and ignore the misleading messages around us.

For example, dozens of times, as part of getting a health history from my clients, I have asked people who smoked if they thought smoking was a good idea. I've never had somebody say, "Yeah, I think smoking is a good idea." We really do know the difference between what is good for us and what is not.

The challenge in such a situation is to avoid justifying,

with all kinds of equivocation and blaming, that which we have chosen despite knowing it to be harmful. Much of the pain we feel could be avoided if we just took responsibility for our own actions and gave our choices the proper name. People ask me all the time, how can I change? How can I know what to do?

My advice is to consider your choices and honestly name the feeling each choice brings. After you have done that, listen to the Spirit, which will tell you, in effect, whether you are "hot" or "cold." The direction you go is your choice, but if you wish to find the hidden peace you seek, my advice would be: Choose hot.

THE SWEETNESS OF SHARING

One of the greatest choices we can make in our lives is the choice to give. Loving and serving others inevitably places us in a position to feel our Father's love. Observing those actions in others provides a testament to the power of our desire, as God's children, to be like him. Many good people feel the desire to give in spite of earthly parental or other examples that are less than service oriented.

I watched a Relief Society president pick one of the busiest days of the year, a holiday, to take a meal to the family of a sister who had cancer. She prepared the kind of meal she thought the family deserved on a special day in such challenging times. The energy and thoughtfulness that took—her desire for goodness—was astounding. She had a bunch of kids of her own and a husband to care for as well. They didn't have the food budget available to eat the same quality of food she took to her neighbors. After a brief discussion they all knowingly gave the better part.

What loving service, not only from her, but from her family, who supported her! They made their sacrifice willingly. She and her husband and the kids who were home unitedly delivered the meal, experiencing the joy of giving and learning a valuable lesson about spiritual nutrition in the process.

When they got home, they were greeted by an unexpected miracle of their own. A feast was set out on their own table, waiting for their return. One of the other women in the Relief Society and two of her best friends had observed the president's kindness and knew what was happening. They had taken the time to do the very thing for her that she had done for her good sister with cancer. In the end, five families were fed and blessed.

Loving and its attendant blessings of giving and receiving are about paying attention to our needs and the needs of others. Sometimes we're in need whether it is apparent to others or not. Sometimes the sweetest blessings come not when we are in physical need but when our needs are spiritual. Maybe we just need somebody to know that we exist, that we are good, and that we are trying. Don't be afraid to call a friend just to let them know you need to talk for a minute or two. Don't be afraid to give or receive the blessing of a kind word or a smile. These opportunities to share are there more often than most of us are willing to believe, if we just look.

Perhaps the greatest gift of giving and receiving is the reminder it provides that we belong to a loving heavenly family.

WHAT WE DO COUNTS

There is a parable in section 101 of the Doctrine and Covenants that helps me understand why obeying and serving and making wise choices are so important. In the parable, the master instructs his servants, in effect: "I want to build an orchard here; it is choice land. Plant twelve trees and then build a hedge around them. I want you to have watchmen circling the hedge to protect the project. After that, build a tower and put a watchman on the tower. If the bad guys come, we will see them from the tower. Because we have seen them in time, we will have a chance to get our defenses ready." With those instructions, the landowner leaves and the servants begin the project. They plant the trees, prepare the hedge, and build the foundation of the tower. We can pick up the story here:

"And while they were yet laying the foundation thereof, they began to say among themselves: And what need hath my lord of this tower? And consulted for a long time, saying among themselves: What need hath my lord of this tower, seeing this is a time of peace? Might not this money be given to the exchangers? For there is no need of these things" (D&C 101:47–49).

As the workers are trying to solve the problem of whether to build the tower or not, the enemy comes and destroys the orchard.

Notice, the workers were not trying to do anything bad here. They were trying to make a return on their employer's investment. After the destruction, the master came back and sadly asked them why they didn't just do what he had asked them to.

At this point in the parable, an interesting lesson came to me. What if, like so many good people in the Church, we do the right thing and build the tower. Sometime during the process we might even question why we are building it, just as the workers in the parable did. But faith wins out. We don't always feel good about it, because constructing a tower is really hard work, but we build it as instructed.

We might say or think things like "This is sure a lot of work," or "Why am I always the one that has to work on building the stupid tower?" Similarly, one of our kids might ask why they can't date until they're sixteen, and that is not an easy conversation to have with a worthy son or daughter. But we are obedient. We build the tower and we stand our watch. Then someone says, "I don't see any bad guys. This is a time of peace. Where is the harm? Why you gotta be so churchy about stuff? I told you we didn't need a tower." The problem we are faced with is we can't say for sure which bad guys didn't come because . . . they saw the tower there and didn't come.

What we ought to be saying is something like this: "Oh, my gosh, isn't this great? Because we had a tower, the bad guys didn't come." In my experience, we don't say that very often.

We don't say it because it isn't always possible to link cause and effect perfectly. We have a hard time linking some of the good outcomes in our lives to our obedience. In fact, this happens all the time. We make the effort to do the right thing, and because we can't connect it to a specific positive outcome, it's hard to see how valuable all our positive effort was.

This inability to make the connection can make our greatest accomplishments seem meaningless. We see our blessings as just some serendipitous gift or lucky break. At the same time, the adversary is yelling in our ear that every bad thing that happens is evidence of our unworthiness or incompetence or our Father's lack of care for us. We see all the blame and none of the benefit.

For example, we often hear this plea in our closing prayers: "Take us home in safety." It has become almost cliché. Nonetheless, it is a prayer that is often answered. When was the last time you returned home from church and prayed, "Heavenly Father, thank you for answering our prayer by taking us all home in safety"?

A young woman might say, "So I'm sixteen and I can date. Well, I waited and what did it change? See, Mom, I'm sixteen and nothing happened. I could have dated at fifteen and a half and been fine." We don't know if that is true, but all our efforts seem unnecessary because we can't connect the child's safety directly with her obedience.

When was the last time I knelt down and said, "Father, I'm thankful I didn't get the cancer I would have been diagnosed with last Wednesday if I had not been living the Word of Wisdom"? We don't know what the bad guys would have done had they not been kept away by the tower. If we ask to be okay, and we are, it's like building the tower and the bad guys not coming. But because we can't make a direct connection, we don't think any more of it. Our acts of faithful obedience seem unrewarded.

The reverse of this is also true. Bad things happen sometimes, no matter how well we prepare. The natural condition of our environment makes it impossible for us not to be affected by the choices of others and by our separation from Father. We forget this principle and believe that we must have done something wrong if our lives are not perfect.

When we experience trials, we begin to believe that we have not done enough, or that what we are doing isn't working. Reading our scriptures, saying our prayers every day, being a good person—those don't count because we don't attach them to any specific positive outcome. It actually takes a huge amount of energy and faith to maintain that standard of obedience, but we think that because of this trial or that challenge, it must not be working. Never mind the 856 blessings in our lives.

Most often the sisters of the Church in particular seem not to feel any satisfaction in a level of performance that the world would call exceptional. This is due in part to some idea that this level of performance is just "what is expected." Perhaps that is true. I am sure the Father had great confidence that the Savior would complete his mission perfectly. That's what was expected. But I am also sure that his mission was infinitely demanding and painful, no matter what he expected of himself or what the Father expected.

Sadly, what we might think of as the "expected" level of performance is not always met in the world. Not everyone loves his children. Not everyone says her prayers. Not everyone tries hard to be good visiting or home teachers. Not every home is a safe place to be. We need to give ourselves credit for the good things we do.

Many of the blessings in our lives are not only a natural consequence of our good choices, but also a monument to our commitment to be obedient. There is a reason to choose the right. Our blessings are not just serendipity or some cosmic door prize we were lucky enough to get.

I'm not saying that every person who builds a tower is always safe from the bad guys. But what I *am* saying is this: If we do what Heavenly Father asks us to, we are safer than if we don't. This is true even if we can't connect cause and effect. This parable is an important reminder that we are safer when we are obedient to God's will, even if we don't know which bad guys we kept away.

In short, if you want to be happy, obey. Build the tower. Follow the Spirit. Taste the sweetness of serving others. These will all help us in our quest to get the most out of life.

CHAPTER 10

How Do We Know How We're Doing?

I worked for several years with a man who taught me much about knowing myself. He was the strongest person, in terms of weight-to-strength ratio, that I have ever known. He seemed to thrive on the challenge of extreme sports. He climbed El Capitan in the Yosemite Valley several times. (That's straight up!) He rode his mountain bike everywhere. He was a returned missionary and a student of the scriptures, an incredibly focused and gifted guy. A master of martial arts, he went to Taiwan just to study karate. His hands were hardened with literally inches of calluses because he was always beating on bricks, beating on wood, beating on planks. He was an amazing character.

He lifted weights and did his exercises every day and was always in training. I was amazed at his discipline, skill, and concentration. I assumed he would be prepared for any kind of physical confrontation. So I asked him, "What would be the coolest thing you could do to use your skill in karate?"

He said, "Oh, I've thought about that many times, and it really motivates me to improve. Here is how I picture a situation that would prove I have arrived as a fighter:

"I want to be in a long line at the movie theater on my first date with a beautiful girl. I want all my friends, everyone from my ward, and my parents and siblings to be there. We're in the line, we've gotten our tickets, ready to go into the movie, and it's sold out. I want a sophomore or junior in high school who is really out of shape and all pimply and adolescent to come up and push me in the chest and say, 'Give me your tickets.' And I want to give them to him."

He stopped, rather pleased with himself, and looked at me as if I should get it.

"That's the whole story?" I asked.

"That's it," he said. "I want to give him my tickets. I want to be so okay with who I am that it doesn't matter what happens or who sees it. There would have been no good reason to hurt the foolish boy. I would know I could have beaten him; that's all that matters. There is no reason to be embarrassed by our choices if we make good ones."

I have contemplated his response over the years. I have come to realize how much pain we could avoid if we only knew who we are and what we value. My friend's greatest desire was to be sure about himself. He wanted to know that there would be no embarrassment, no lack of face in just saying, "Take the tickets."

When I have been tempted to make a big issue over a little thing, this thought has come to me: "Give him the tickets." There are enough meaningful battles in life to fight. I ought to save my strength for those and not waste it on the little skirmishes.

STRAWBERRY JAM

One of the biggest battles we face in life is letting go of our guilt. Even after we have made changes and sought the forgiveness of our Father in Heaven, sometimes we can't seem to let go.

When Lois and I were in school, we agreed with our next-door neighbors to invest all our money to buy strawberries and make strawberry jam. We cleaned and mashed berries and put in the sugar and pectin. We made this huge, tall, pressure-canner pot full of hot strawberry mush. It was cooking on the stove and we were just having a great time when my buddy caught his sleeve on the pot and pulled it off the stove. It didn't tip over but hit flat on the floor and just splashed. In just a few careless seconds, our lives changed. We spent four or five hours cleaning strawberry jam off everything. It didn't all spill out of the pot, and we did get some jam, but the day was a mess. I remember how long that one incident took us to clean up.

In fact, about two and a half years later, when I graduated and we moved out of that little apartment, we were still finding little flecks of that strawberry jam.

That's an interesting analogy for getting over the messes in our lives. Sometimes we make mistakes that will change everything in just a few seconds. Those mistakes may take us all kinds of time to clean up. But there are a couple of important lessons to be learned. Lesson number one is: The longer you wait to clean up a mess, the worse it gets. If we hadn't taken three or four hours right at the time of the mistake, when it was still relatively easy to clean, it would have been horrible. Every time anybody walked through, they could have tracked jam all over the house.

Lesson number two: Even after we think we have taken care of a mess, it seems to pop up again. From time to time, no matter how hard we have cleaned, we'll find a fleck of berry jam in an unexpected place. Then, rather than saying, "See, I can never be forgiven," or "It's everywhere in my life," or "I'll never be as good as everybody else," we can say: "I can't believe how many places that jam was! I'm so glad it's cleaned up; let me just wipe this little piece away. It doesn't matter anymore."

That is a very interesting lesson. Clean as we will, we're going to encounter a moment or two in our lives when we are reminded of our mistake. We'll find a piece of it somewhere unexpected. The important thing to remember is that once we've done the cleanup, everything after that is just a reminder to be careful. That occasional reminder is a safety precaution that can make us glad that mess is behind us and grateful that it can keep us from making other messes.

Looking Back to See How Far You Have Come

One of the things we need to be reminded of on a daily basis is where we are relative to where we've been, not just relative to where we are headed. I don't know how you feel, but where we are headed—perfection— seems a long way off some days. My problem is, when I look from day to day, that destination of perfection doesn't seem to be getting any closer.

Let me give you an example of what I mean. There is a creek I love to fish, a high-mountain, brook-trout stream. To get there I park my truck, get all my gear on, and then have to walk about two miles. It is steep country, and the climb takes me up and through a little saddle between two peaks. As soon as I crest the ridge, the trail drops sharply. There, maybe two hundred and fifty yards below, is a big, open meadow. That high, hanging valley is one of my favorite places on earth, and it is beautiful. After I get there, it always feels worth it. Sometimes, before I make it to the top and look down, I wonder.

You may ask yourself, "Why is he complaining about a trip he wants to make?" I know I want to go, but that doesn't make it easier. I live at sea level, and the spot where I get out of the truck is at an elevation of about 7,600 feet. For a chubby guy from sea level, that is no-air, nosebleed high. One of the things I love is that it is so clear and so high and so beautiful. One of the hard things is the two-mile hike up this really steep trail in that high, thin air before I get to my gorgeous destination.

I set my sights on the little saddle on the mountain, knowing that if I can get through there, I will have some wonderful fishing and a really great day. So it seems worth it, at first. Then the climb begins. I walk and walk and walk and walk. I walk forever. Then I look up at the saddle, and I think, *It is no closer than it was when I left the truck!* It seems so far, and I'm out of breath, and it's so hard, and it's not getting any closer. Best of all, if I quit the trail, the walk back to the truck is all downhill.

What I have to do, at this point of tempting despair, is turn around and look at the truck. When I do, I get a new perspective. I've come a long way. In that clear mountain air, the goal is pretty clear, but it's farther away than it looks. Only by checking where I've been can I understand how far I've come toward where I really want to go.

Sometimes we keep our eyes so focused on the prize—which is important—that we forget to recognize: "You know what, I'm better off than I was a month ago. I am doing better. I'm kinder than I was a year ago. I'm a better husband than I was six months ago. I'm a better mom than I used to be."

The gift here is to recognize that the journey can be joyful. Think of the discovery, not just the enduring. Think of the ride, not just the destination. Once in a while, as an added bonus, when I look back I am treated to a vista that is surprising in its beauty.

Here is a fun exercise to illustrate further. Open your scriptures and look at all the red marks, or blue marks, or whatever marks you use. The thing that really encourages me when I do that is the thought: *Look at all those marks; I must have done some studying.* I know that at some point I read what is marked. I've put in some hours trying to learn and grow. Even though the prize of perfect scriptural understanding might seem like it's a far, far piece away, I've certainly made progress.

Sometimes perfection, or getting it all right, feels so huge that we feel that no matter how far up the trail we go, we're never getting closer. That is not true. The best part is that if we recognize the effort and growth we *have* made, it reminds us that we are still firmly on the trail.

How Will We Know If We Are Winners?

One of my most memorable life lessons about change and choice came from my experience with a high school football team. Their coach was a dear friend who asked me to come in and help him teach his new team about winning. He was a retired high school teacher. He had been and still was a great football coach. Most important, he was a builder of young people.

My friend had taken the job knowing that the program was on the ropes. They hadn't won many football games in several years. In fact, as I recall, the year before he arrived, the team was winless. As the new head coach, he brought both the staff and the system with him. This was not his first chance to build a program. He had great confidence in his staff and his system. He knew the system would work as soon as the young men believed in themselves. So he asked me, as a member of the community, if I would help these young men learn how to win.

I joined them at training camp that August to be introduced and to lead a very lively discussion about why they were such losers. I suggested several theories.

Perhaps the school boundaries had been drawn with football-related genetics in mind. Did they believe that somehow some secret conspiracy had managed to get all the inferior athletes put into the same high school? They were vocally dismayed at that theory.

I then suggested that there might be a drinking-water problem in their area that caused a lack of athletic vigor among the students. That idea was also rejected. I then invited suggestions from them as to why the school had a history of football failure. Again, a lively debate followed. They decided that the school had a habit of losing.

Essentially no one, including the players, really thought they could win. They suggested that some of the best athletes participated in other fall sports because they did not want to play football and lose.

I let them know that the coaching staff had built programs and won state championships. The system and the staff were proven, committed, and ready. If we rejected my genetics or water theories, and we all did, all that remained as a question mark was them. I promised them that if they listened to the coaching staff, followed the program, and just did their best, they would win. Would they commit to working hard enough to learn to win? They said they would. I said if they would, then so would I.

I committed to the sophomores that I would attend every game until they graduated. I told them I was not being paid for my help. I did want one thing from them as payment, however. I wanted to know from them, after every game they played for those three years, whether or not they had done their best.

Here is how they would let me know. I would stand at the end of the field as they came off. If they had given their best, they were to give me a high-five on the way out. If they hadn't, for whatever reason, all I wanted them to say on their way past me was, "I'll do better." Either way, I asked them to look me in the eye and report how they evaluated their performance. That was all.

I also committed to come to the preparation meal the

night before each game and share a positive thought or two. The night before every game, the moms and dads put a good meal together and the team watched football high-light films. This was a carbo-load dinner sponsored by the booster club to build team morale and unity.

I knew the coach and his program and had great confidence in the system. I knew if the boys would believe in the program and in themselves, they would win a lot of football games.

It was during one of those Thursday night meals that a member of the team posed a very thought-provoking question. He raised his hand and asked, "Mr. Nelson, how are we going to know when we've become winners? How will we know if we have changed?" This was not just a team question but an individual one. It was a great question, and I asked for a week to think my answer over. I thought about his question all week. I reviewed a hundred possible ways to measure a change in attitude.

I decided that the best barometer of whether real change had taken place would be reflected in the team member's first thought when he was faced with a potential challenge. "If an assumed positive outcome is your first thought," I told him the next week, "then you have changed." Then I used the following example to illustrate the point.

Let's say you recover a fumble on your own five-yard line. If your first thought is, "Oh, man, we've got a long way to go," or, "We just dodged a bullet," you're still not there. But if your first thought—I mean your *very* first thought—is, "Awesome, we get to drive for a 95-yard touchdown," then you'll know you have changed.

"When it happens," I said, "and it will, I will be standing where I always stand on the top right of the bleachers watching. When a winning thought is your first thought in adversity, you turn and point to me in the stands and smile, and I'll know."

The next year in a tough game about halfway through the season, they recovered a fumble on their own one-yard line. Most of them recognized at once what a real opportunity it would be for them to drive 99 yards to get a touchdown. A number of players turned and looked at me in the stands and pointed as part of their celebration. It was a rare moment in my life. They knew they had changed. They had become winners. They saw the opportunity, not the obstacle. You couldn't have stopped those boys with a bomb. As soon as they recovered that fumble, they knew they were going to drive down for the touchdown. That was when many of them knew for the first time that they were champions. They had come to know that in adversity is opportunity. They had come to believe in their ability to weather the storms of life.

Those sophomores finished second in the state their senior year—they were beaten in the final game by a "Hail Mary" pass with sixteen seconds to go. That season was the gift that faith and commitment had given a bunch of boys who three years earlier were winless. It was a wonderful experience, and they enjoyed every minute of it. It was fun to watch as they, along with their parents and the student body, learned what was possible for winners.

Those young men graduated proud of themselves and of what they had accomplished on the field. Only a couple went on to play college football, but every one of them had learned how to win. They went on as winners who knew that if you pay the price, you get your chance.

Life is like that football team. We are not very different from those around us. Success in the things that truly matter in life isn't really a matter of genetics or luck. We become champions if we can learn to see opportunity instead of adversity. If we can learn to see a chance instead of a roadblock, we will prosper. If we learn to work hard and assume we are going to be okay, we will have better lives.

That change in perspective and the motivation to do the hard work that goes along with it will give us more confidence. Accepting the confidence and support of a good coaching staff and a proven system is what it takes to change our level of confidence and commitment. It changes our assumptions from hopeless to happy. When we take that attitude and build a partnership with Heavenly Father, our winning is assured. There is no better coach and no better system. The good news is that he is always looking for players willing to learn to become champions.

We can all be winners. Every one of us kept our first estate. We all have the potential, with the help of our loving Father, to keep our second estate as well. Take time to look back once in a while and see how far you've come. Believe that you can make it the rest of the way and that the eternal view will be worth it.

We Can Change the World

*F*or many of us, the idea that we have a loving and supportive Father in Heaven who cares about us and has confidence in us is at first almost incomprehensible. Our life experience and what we have been taught are so different from that. Add to that his invitation to come to him and accept him as a loving partner in this earthly enterprise, even if our performance has been less than perfect, and it seems too good to be true. It is not. He is our Father, and he loves us in the same way we love our own families, but perfectly.

It takes great faith to believe this at first. But after we have gained enough understanding to test these assertions, our faith can grow into hope and finally become knowledge. It is worth the risk of testing to come to this knowledge. In Alma 32, beginning in verse 26, the testing process is described in detail and compared to a growing seed. I love the description of how it feels to come to a knowledge of the goodness of the seed. The scripture says, "It must needs be that this is a good seed, or that the word is good, for it beginneth to enlarge my soul; yea, it beginneth to enlighten my understanding, yea, it beginneth to be delicious to me" (v. 28).

Take this chance to believe that God's love for us is real and available. Believe that we can, with our gift of agency, choose to know him and become more like him. Believe that we can live our lives in such a way as to find peace in spite of our earthly trials. Believe that in the end we can say, as Paul did to Timothy, "I have fought a good fight, I have finished my course, I have kept the faith: Henceforth there is laid up for me a crown of righteousness, which the Lord, the righteous judge, shall give me at that day: and not to me only, but unto all them also that love his appearing" (2 Timothy 4:7–8).

There is a wonderful story in Arthurian legend that describes this test of trust and faith beautifully. The story is about an island called Avalon. The beautiful island of Avalon sat peacefully in the middle of a great inland sea. Avalon was unlike the rest of the world. During the time of King Arthur, the world was a dark and evil place, much as it seems now, but Avalon was a place of beauty and peace. This island was a place where there were no monsters. There were no dragons, no wicked kings or queens, no sorcerers, no poisonous serpents—there was no evil there, and none could ever be there.

There was a problem in finding Avalon, however. The island was always surrounded by impenetrable mists. The mists of Avalon protected the pure in heart; they kept the island secure from evil.

Those protective mists parted to reveal the island and provide sanctuary only for those who truly believed the island was there even without seeing it. You had to row toward an island you could not be sure was there. Unless you had the faith to put in this effort, it remained hidden.

However, as you went forth in confidence, the mists would part and soon you would be safely there. Such is the power of faith in something or some Being that really exists in spite of the veil that separates us.

I believe the mists and Avalon are analogous to the love of God and the Savior and the great plan of happiness. As soon as we overcome the lies and distractions that Satan uses to keep us from believing in our Father's affection, we begin to be hopeful. With that hope comes faith and then charity. When we experience the fruits of our experiment, the mists part, and we go to a place without monsters.

The power of our choice is the key to revealing the truth. Maybe you've played the little imagining game I like to call "In My World." It's a game Latter-day Saints play about reaching the celestial kingdom and beginning to create their own eternal environments. It is a game that expresses faith in the eventual saving power of the great plan of happiness.

In my experience, it is played most often by women and starts usually something like this: "In my world, chocolate will be calorie free." "In my world, all the men will be [you can fill in the blank]." "In my world . . . "

What I pray we will understand is that we have our choice and agency here and now. *This* is our world. We can make the best of this place by making good choices. We can't change physical laws—I can't make chocolate calorie free. I can't make all the other people in my world dependable. But I can say this about the part of the world I am responsible for:

"In my world, I will feel the love of our Heavenly Father.

"In my world, when I go to church I will seek the Spirit and renew my covenants in good conscience.

"In my world, there are still good people.

"In my world, everybody is going to have value.

"In my world, little girls are safe.

"In my world, I will measure the things I know Heavenly Father is measuring and treat myself and others appropriate to those measures."

Now that's even better than chocolate! And I guarantee you that when the love of our Heavenly Father is allowed to penetrate the mists we've built or allowed to be placed around our hearts, we can not only appreciate our children, we can appreciate being children of God. Such feelings will turn our spirits to Avalon, a place with no monsters.

Index

discontent, 37; physical
problems of, 81; on
concentrating your efforts
on what matters most, 87
McKay, David O., on acting your
part, 76

Navajo: experience with
medicine man, 57–59;
experience walking into
hogan, 90–91
Nonmember husband:
experience with baptism of,
69–71; experience receiving
priesthood blessing from
former, 71–73

Obedience: parable of the
servants and the tower,
131–33; difficulty of linking
good outcomes to, 133–34;
danger of assuming bad
outcomes are the result of
poor performance, 134–35;
recognizing the blessings of,
135–36

Parables: lost girl, 16–19;
training wheels, 19–23;
talents, 27–30; pointing
finger, 57–59; servants and
the tower, 131–33
Peck, M. Scott, on missing the
gift of God's grace, 64–65
Perspective: dangers of a narrow,
122; looking at the entire
picture, 123; adopting an
eternal, 123–24
Peterson, Melvin, 104
Physical constraints: as a
consequence of life in a

fallen place, 79; recognizing
psychological problems as
physical ailments, 79–81; as
experienced by Spencer W.
Kimball and Neal A.
Maxwell, 81; schizophrenia,
81–82; depression, 82–83;
lessening the impact of
psychological problems,
83–84; experience with
exhausted young mother,
84–85; virtuous exhaustion,
84–88; avoiding the trap of
"the more we do, the better
God likes us," 85–86;
Neal A. Maxwell on
concentrating your efforts
on what matters most, 87;
listening to the advice you
would give as a parent,
87–88
Plain and precious things,
appreciating, 92–93
Pointing finger, parable of the,
57–59
Practicing for recital, experience
with mother of friend, 75
Prayer: experience offering only
prayers of gratitude, 99–100;
experience receiving
counsel from stake
presidency member on sin
and, 102–3. See also
"Seminary answer"
Premortal life: basis of war in
heaven, 7; what Satan wants
you to believe about, 7–8;
presentation of God's plan
of happiness, 8–10; Satan's
rebellion, 10–11;